PRESENTED TO:

FROM:

DEVOTIONS *for* EVERY DAY *of the* YEAR

His

PARABLES

The MOST MOVING WORDS EVER WRITTEN
ABOUT *the* PARABLES *of* JESUS

INTEGRITY®
PUBLISHERS

Produced with the assistance of The Livingstone Corporation (www.LivingstoneCorp.com). Introductions written by Neil Wilson. Project staff includes David Veerman, Linda Taylor, Ashley Taylor, Kirk Luttrell, Andy Culbertson, Phoebe Blaustein, Don Jones, Sara Jones, David Thompson, David Eyk, Nathan White, Terefe Bolteno, Teri Hill, Erika Godfrey, Tom Ristow, and Kathy Ristow.

Cover and Interior Design: Brand Navigation, LLC. www.brandnavigation.com

Cover and Interior Images: Pixelworks Studio, Steve Gardner

ISBN 1-59145-270-8

Printed in China

05   06   07   08   09   RRD   10 9 8 7 6 5 4 3 2 1

TABLE OF CONTENTS

INTRODUCTION

I n the pages that follow you will be exposed to the stories Jesus told. Beware.

Jesus' parables are like Trojan horses grazing peacefully on the vast plains of the Internet. They seem like harmless strands of narrative until we let them loose inside our programming. Then they wreak havoc. Simple objects and actions take on gigantesque proportions. The little metaphors about the kingdom of God turn out to be larger than life. If we download the seed-messages, we eventually discover that they produce a huge tree whose roots extend to every dark corner of our hidden life and cast shade over the entire landscape of our existence.

Two thousand years of Christian thought have not plumbed the depths of Jesus' teaching. Every generation seems destined to rediscover the power in the parables. The selections you are about to read will be testimonies to the radical effects of these deceptively simple word-pictures and stories. The changes you are about to undergo will be good for you. They might even turn you into a living parable.

WHY
PARABLES?

---

*The disciples came to him and asked,
"Why do you speak to the
people in parables?"*

MATTHEW 13:10 NIV

WHY PARABLES?

Jesus told stories. He connected with people. They flocked to Him for healing and for hearing. Jesus, as only a Creator would, understood something basic about human nature. We love stories because we are stories. Each of us is a central character in a narrative of our own. We have an Author, but we are conscious characters in our story. When we hear Jesus' parables, we remember similar scenes from our life. We are invited to understand something new by laying it alongside something old.

At a certain point in His life, Matthew tells us, Jesus spoke to people almost exclusively in parables. Multitudes listened to those stories, but they seldom understood. They were drawn to the storyteller but wondered about His purpose. Their confusion raises a significant question: was the problem that they didn't understand the stories or that they didn't understand why He told them?

In the readings that follow, wrestle along with other minds over the purpose of Jesus' parables and the difference between unbelief and ignorance.

UNDERSTANDING PARABLES

MATTHEW 13:10 ESV
Then the disciples came and said to him,
"Why do you speak to them in parables?"

The parable is essentially a sword to stab men's minds awake; and therefore its interpretation can never be that which could be discovered only after long labour in the study. It must be that one single truth the story illuminates which leaps out to meet the listener's mind. . . . The parable was originally spoken by Jesus to illustrate one aspect of truth, to stress that particular aspect of the truth which the need of the moment required. To take an example: it is quite wrong to find the whole of Christian theology in the parable of the Prodigal Son and to forget that there are parables of judgment and *vice versa*. But if we remember that the situation in which a parable was spoken will always shed a flood of light on its meaning, and that in every case Jesus is throwing into bold relief one aspect of the truth, then when we put the parables all together we shall gain an unmatched insight into the mind of the Master Teacher.

WILLIAM BARCLAY

HEARING AND DOING

MARK 4:33 NIV
*With many similar parables Jesus spoke the word
to them, as much as they could understand.*

Shocking is, first of all, the sharp distinction between
those outside and the inner circle of the disciples. . . .
Who is "in"? Those who understand the secrets of the
Kingdom of God and—not to be overlooked—who
change their ways. For both belong inseparably together in Jesus' eyes. The doing is always the proof of
the hearing.

What does it mean to understand the secrets of the
Kingdom of God? Jesus doubtless refers to His own
words; even more, He refers to the presence of God in His
person, in His Word, and in His deeds. This is the separa-
tion between those outside and those inside: The latter
have understood who He is and that God is creating a
new life in them, and the former have not. This understanding is totally different from what we may learn
through religious instruction, through theological studies
or the reading of books. . . . Doing is the true measure of
understanding.

EMIL BRUNNER

SPEAKING IN PICTURES

MATTHEW 13:35 NKJV
*. . . that it might be fulfilled which was spoken
by the prophet, saying: "I will open My mouth
in parables; I will utter things kept secret
from the foundation of the world."*

What then are the parables, if they are not alle-
gories? They are the natural expression of a mind
that sees truth in concrete pictures rather than conceives
it in abstractions. . . . This concrete, pictorial mode of
expression is thoroughly characteristic of the sayings of
Jesus. Thus instead of saying, "Beneficence should not be
ostentatious," He says, "When you give alms, do not blow
your trumpet;" instead of saying, "Wealth is a grave hindrance to true religion," He says, "It is easier for a camel
to go through the eye of a needle than for a rich man to
enter the Kingdom of God." In such figurative expressions the germ of the parable is already present.

C. H. DODD

THE PURPOSE OF PARABLES

ISAIAH 32:3 NASB

Then the eyes of those who see will not be blinded,
And the ears of those who hear will listen.

Since the reader or audience is left to unravel the meaning and application, a knowledge of both the setting and the intended audience of a parable is important to the interpretation of the figurative speech forms. . . . And most often, the intended audience is not a homogeneous crowd, but consists of a mix of so-called insiders and outsiders. That is, people with a listening ear and obedient heart (i.e., the insider, cf. Isaiah 32:1–8; 50:4–5) and people with blind eyes, deaf ears, and a rebellious spirit (i.e., the outsider, cf. Isaiah 42:18–25; 48:8).

The parable may be akin to the riddle at times, in that the mysterious nature and foolish character of this figurative speech form is both *clue* and *snare* to the audience. Hence, the literary purposes of the parable are often directly related to the directness or obscurity of the symbolic language employed.

ANDREW HILL

THE FAITH OF A CHILD

MARK 9:36 NKJV
*Then He took a little child and set him in
the midst of them. And when He had taken
him in His arms, He said to them . . .*

There is a culture of sarcasm that has for decades filtered down from our media and many of our leaders to infect all of us. I've often said that I don't see how a committed follower of Christ can maintain a sarcastic approach to humor, but we have so few other models before us. . . . Cynicism is a deadly infection that eats away our childlike ability to be surprised and delighted. It corrodes our channel of worship, and that disease is a terminal one.

It's not a new problem, of course. Jesus faced the cynics at every turn. Not only were the Pharisees incapable of partaking in the marvelous experience of His miracles and teaching, but even His own disciples constantly fell short of the grand concept. So many of His parables invited the hearers to wonder at the greatness of the kingdom of God, but nearly everyone missed the point. Finally, since they couldn't see the big picture, He gave them the small one. He held up a little child.

DAVID JEREMIAH

PARABLES AND THE WORD

HEBREWS 4:12 NRSV

*Indeed, the word of God is living and active,
sharper than any two-edged sword, piercing until it
divides soul from spirit, joints from marrow; it is able
to judge the thoughts and intentions of the heart.*

Scripture, as we have seen, is a many-sided interpretive record of an intricate cross-section of world history. The Word of God is an exceedingly complex unity. The different items and the various kinds of material which make it up—laws, promises, liturgies, genealogies, arguments, narratives, meditations, visions, aphorisms, homilies, parables, and the rest—do not stand in Scripture as isolated fragments, but as parts of a whole. The exposition of them, therefore, involves exhibiting them in right relation both to the whole and to each other. God's Word is not presented in Scripture in the form of a theological system. But it admits of being stated in that form, and, indeed, requires to be so stated before we can properly grasp it—grasp it, that is, as a whole.

J. I. PACKER

EVERYDAY LIFE

HEBREWS 4:12 NIV
For the word of God is living and active.

Virtually the first thing we notice about the parables is their everyday realism and concrete vividness. . . . The parables take us right into the familiar world of planting and harvesting, traveling through the countryside, baking bread, tending sheep, or responding to an invitation. The parables thus obey the literary principle of verisimilitude ("lifelikeness"), and a perusal of commentaries always uncovers new evidence of how thoroughly rooted in real life the parables are. . . .

This minute realism is an important part of the meaning of Jesus' parables. On the surface, these stories are totally "secular." There are few overtly religious activities in the parables. If we approached them without their surrounding context and pretended that they were anonymous, we could not guess that they were intended for a religious purpose. An important by-product of this realism is that it undermines the "two-world" thinking in which the spiritual and earthly spheres are rigidly divided. We are given to understand that it is in everyday experience that spiritual decisions are made and that God's grace does its work.

LELAND RYKEN

WHAT IS A PARABLE?

*Jesus used this figure of speech with them, but they
did not understand what he was saying to them.*

Parables were not similes—stories using "as" or "like"
that took a truth and made an exact replica as in "To
what shall I liken this generation?" Parables were not
metaphors or implied comparisons like "I am the Vine,
and you are the branches." Parables were not hyperbole,
or intentional exaggeration, such as "faith like a mustard
seed."

A parable—meaning "to throw alongside"—was a
story that delivered a parallel truth. It was a pithy, fictional
story that had one purpose: to underscore the point of the
message. St. Augustine, when he was teaching his students
how to interpret Scripture, said that there were three keys
to doing so: context, context, and context. The three
most important elements of dynamic communication are
illustration, illustration, and illustration. And the form of
illustration that Jesus used most often was the parable.

R. C. SPROUL AND ROBERT WOLGEMUTH

EVERYONE LOVES A STORY

2 TIMOTHY 3:16 NLT

*All Scripture is inspired by God and is useful
to teach us what is true and to make us realize
what is wrong in our lives. It straightens us
out and teaches us to do what is right.*

Everyone loves a good story. Public speakers know that stories effectively illustrate their points. Grandfathers, like me, know that stories are often the great connector between generations. "Papa, read me a story," is so compelling that I drop everything to obey. When one of my grandkids is nestled on my lap and I'm reciting something from the printed page, all is well with the world, and I am at peace.

Jesus knew that telling stories would be a profound way of connecting with an audience, illuminating truth, and building relationships. And so He told stories . . . parables.

R. C. SPROUL AND ROBERT WOLGEMUTH

HOPE

ROMANS 15:4 KJV
For whatsoever things were written aforetime were written for our learning, that we through patience and comfort of the scriptures might have hope.

One spiritual writer has observed that human beings are born with two diseases: life, from which we die; and hope, which says the first disease is not terminal. Hope is built into the structure of our personalities, into the depths of our unconscious; it plagues us to the very moment of our death. The critical question is whether hope is self-deception, the ultimate cruelty of a cruel and tricky universe, or whether it is just possibly the imprint of reality.

The parables of Jesus respond to that question. In effect Jesus says: Hope your wildest hopes, dream your maddest dreams, imagine your most fantastic fantasies. Where your hopes and your dreams and your imagination leave off, the love of my heavenly Father only begins. For "eye hath not seen, nor ear heard, neither have entered into the heart of man, the things which God hath prepared for them that love him" (1 Corinthians 2:9 KJV).

BRENNAN MANNING

THE SUBTLE STORYTELLER

MATTHEW 13:3 ESV
And he told them many things in parables . . .

Jesus provides a striking example of one skilled in the art of storytelling. Like most of his Jewish forebears and contemporaries, when Jesus was asked questions he did not respond by reasoning from a starting point to a conclusion. Rather, he usually replied by telling a story, often in the form of a parable. By this method he engaged his audience, that is, he got them involved in arriving at the answer in a vivid and personal way. At the same time, this was how he made his point. The point, however, was usually made subtly, imaginatively, and indirectly. Jesus does not always spell out the truth he is communicating. He allows the one listening to the story to draw his own conclusions. The truth thus comes across in an allusive rather than direct way; it is implicit rather than explicit. By means of this creative approach, the listener usually ends up convicting himself.

MARVIN R. WILSON

GOD IN THE ORDINARY

MATTHEW 21:45 NRSV
*When the chief priests and the Pharisees
heard his parables, they realized that
he was speaking about them.*

Jesus spoke in parables because parables are a form of discourse that have the potential both to image God differently and to open up a wider range of imaginative and volitional responses among listeners and readers than the discourse of law and purity. In other words, Jesus did not respond to his Pharisaic critics *on their own terms*— perhaps because holiness defined in terms of law and cult forecloses prematurely or restricts too narrowly the boundaries of God's mercy and love as embodied in Jesus himself.

Related is the idea that extended parables such as we find in Luke 15 have the potential, by virtue of their very mundane, human, realistic, and subtle character, for revealing "God in the ordinary." Such parables are an invitation to see God and the world differently—that is, to be converted by a divine grace mediated through everyday stories, whose content, on the surface, is quite mundane, but which, for that very reason, paradoxically, brings God near.

STEPHEN C. BARTON

SEEING THROUGH THE EYES
OF OTHERS

2 TIMOTHY 3:16 NIV

*All Scripture is God-breathed and is useful for teaching,
rebuking, correcting and training in righteousness.*

The parables are brilliant verbal constructs, traps for
the unwary. They begin with common things:
workers, masters, mustard seeds. But each parable moves
in a startling way from the familiar to the unfamiliar.
Workers who labor for an hour are paid the same as those
who've worked all day; a despised outsider shows more
compassion for a mugging victim than do members of
God's chosen people.

The parables catch us out, force us to admit our petty,
unimaginative ways of thinking. They cannot be absorbed
passively; we must participate in them. Our response literally completes the story by making it *our* story. . . .

Through the imagination we enact the fundamental
principle that Jesus came to teach: we must learn to see
through the eyes of others. In allowing ourselves to be
transported into the experience of others, art takes us out
of ourselves, teaches us compassion. And because compassion means "suffering with," the imagination has to
take into account the whole of reality, including the existence of evil, death, and human folly.

GREGORY WOLFE

THE SPIRITUAL EAR

LUKE 8:8 ESV
As he said these things, he called out,
"He who has ears to hear, let him hear."

At the end of verse eight Jesus makes sure we got the point about hearing, and says, "He who has ears to hear, let him hear." That means it's not enough to have ears on the side of your head. Everybody has those. But there is another kind of ear that only some people have. And those can hear. "He who has ears to hear, let him hear." There is a spiritual ear, or a heart-ear. There is an ear that hears, in the preaching of the Word, more than mere words. There is a beauty and a truth and a power that these ears hear as compelling and transforming and preserving. That's the kind of hearing Jesus is calling for.

JOHN PIPER

THE GIFT OF UNDERSTANDING

LUKE 8:9–10 NKJV

*Then His disciples asked Him, saying,
"What does this parable mean?" And He said,
"To you it has been given to know the mysteries
of the kingdom of God, but to the rest it is given
in parables, that 'Seeing they may not see,
and hearing they may not understand.'"*

To stress the issue of hearing even more, Luke tells us how Jesus explained the purpose of parables in his situation. In verses 9–10, "His disciples began questioning Him as to what this parable meant. And He said, 'To you it has been granted to know the mysteries of the kingdom of God, but to the rest it is in parables, so that "seeing they may not see, and hearing they may not understand."'" This is a shocking word. To those whom Jesus has chosen, the mystery of His kingdom is opened and He gives them the gift of understanding. Verse 10a: "To you it has been granted to know the mysteries of the kingdom of God." Understanding the kingdom of God is a free gift of God for those whom Jesus has chosen as His disciples.

JOHN PIPER

HEARING WITHOUT UNDERSTANDING

LUKE 8:10 ESV

*He said, "To you it has been given to know
the secrets of the kingdom of God, but for others
they are in parables, so that seeing they may not see,
and hearing they may not understand."*

B ut then [Jesus] says (in verse 10b) that for the others,
the reason for his parables is "so that seeing they may
not see, and hearing they may not understand." The issue
is hearing again. "Hearing they may not understand."
That means there are two kinds of hearing: one with the
physical ears of the head and one with the spiritual ears of
the heart. Hearing (with the physical ears), they do not
understand (with the spiritual ears). And this, He says, is
one of the reasons He uses parables—"so that" hearing,
they may not understand. In other words, the parables are
part of Jesus' concealing and hardening ministry as well as
part of His revealing and saving ministry.

JOHN PIPER

THE MYSTERY OF THE PARABLES

LUKE 8:10 NIV

He said, "The knowledge of the secrets of the
kingdom of God has been given to you, but to others
I speak in parables, so that, 'though seeing, they may
not see; though hearing, they may not understand.'"

To characterize the parables of Jesus as God's picture-book may be somewhat provocative. Are seedtime and harvest, home and the far country, birds and flowers, are all these figures and latitudes of our world actually images of the divine mysteries? Is everything transitory merely a symbol, as Goethe says? If this were so, then it would be possible to read all the mysteries of the eternal from this picture writing of our terrestrial world and perhaps there would be no need for the explanatory word.

And yet the teller of these parables indicates that the lilies of the field and the birds of the air are not simply runes which can be employed to unlock and, as it were, spell out the riddle of our existence. On the contrary, the parables themselves are surrounded with mystery. They can lead—and this may even be their intention—to the listeners' "hearing" but yet not "understanding;" indeed, they may actually drive him to deafness and impenitence.

JOHN W. DOBERSTEIN

HOW JESUS COMMUNICATED

MATTHEW 7:28–29 NLT
After Jesus finished speaking, the crowds were amazed at his teaching, for he taught as one who had real authority—quite unlike the teachers of religious law.

We can learn so much from Jesus, the great teacher. Sometimes he made statements which had air all around them, so to speak; statements which he did not explicitly link with what went before or followed afterwards; statements which on first hearing seemed unconnected or enigmatic. This was because he wanted his hearers to think about what he was saying, to "stretch" for the truth, to work out the deep-level connections for themselves. . . .

He showed great analytical power in his capacity to construct arguments and reason things through. He also demonstrated vividness of imagination. He could see and communicate pictures and images that acted like depth-charges in his hearers, bringing into play their emotions and involving them in situations in a way that analytical reasoning could not do. . . .

Thus, he had any number of ways of making people listen and think. Those of us who aim to be good communicators of Christianity could have no better model than Christ himself.

J. I. PACKER

HIS PARABLES

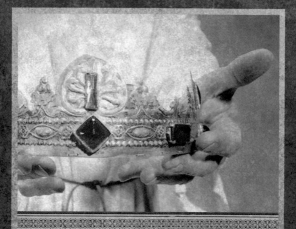

PICTURES OF
THE KINGDOM
OF GOD

"The time has come," he said.
"The kingdom of God is near.
Repent and believe the good news!"
MARK 1:15 NIV

PICTURES OF THE KINGDOM OF GOD

Jesus constantly had the kingdom of God on His mind. He practiced what He preached: "Seek the Kingdom of God above all else, and live righteously, and he will give you everything you need" (Matthew 6:33 NLT). More than any other subject, Jesus devoted His parables to developing a rich collage of the kingdom. Every aspect of life seemed to hold metaphors to illuminate the kingdom. The passage of time has not dimmed the light for those willing to look closely.

From seeds to weeds and soils to treasure, from fishermen to pearl merchants, Jesus dipped His verbal brush into life and painted pictures of Life as it was originally meant to be. In the pages to come you will glance over the shoulders of keen observers to see new views of the kingdom. These humble guides will point out vistas that will take your breath away. Seek the kingdom above all else as you read.

THE SOURCE OF JOY

ROMANS 14:17 NIV
*For the kingdom of God is not a matter
of eating and drinking, but of righteousness,
peace and joy in the Holy Spirit.*

To know that you are loved—that is one source of joy. . . . To feel that nobody cares for me, treats me as a person, or bothers with me, and that I matter to nobody is a great joy-killer. Now the Christian knows love in a way that nobody else does, for he knows that God so loved the world that he gave his only Son to die in shame for us on the cross. . . .

Discontent is another great joy-killer, whereas to accept our situation is a source of joy. Now Christians can always do that because they know that all their circumstances are planned out for them by a loving heavenly Father (Romans 8:28). . . .

Joy comes too from an awareness that we have something worth having. People say, "My spouse, children, home, books, hobbies, and so on are a joy to me." But Paul speaks of "the surpassing worth of knowing Christ Jesus my Lord" (Philippians 3:8).

J. I. PACKER

SECRET GROWTH

MARK 4:26–27 NCV

Then Jesus said, "The kingdom of God is like someone who plants seed in the ground. Night and day, whether the person is asleep or awake, the seed still grows, but the person does not know how it grows."

Jesus told the story of the seed growing in secret (Mark 4:26–29). The seed, once sown, disappears from view. Even though it is germinating and growing beneath the earth, we cannot see this from our limited vantage point above. Only when the growing shoot finally breaks through the soil and announces its presence to the world can we really grasp the fact that, up to that point, it has been growing in secret.

Similarly, we have to face up to the fact that the seed of the gospel takes a long time to break through in our lives. There will be long periods of invisibility, silence, and darkness in our spiritual growth. We have just got to get used to this and realize that it does not imply any weakness or failure on the part of God, or lack of commitment or care on his part . . . but the weak and fallen human nature with which he has to deal.

ALISTER MCGRATH

PATIENCE AND FAITH

MATTHEW 13:24–25 NKJV
Another parable He put forth to them, saying: "The kingdom of heaven is like a man who sowed good seed in his field; but while men slept, his enemy came and sowed tares among the wheat and went his way."

Although Christ has cleansed the Church with his own blood, that it may be without spot or blemish, yet hitherto he suffers it to be polluted by many stains. I speak not of the remaining infirmities of the flesh, to which every believer is liable, even after that he has been renewed by the Holy Spirit. But as soon as Christ has gathered a small flock for himself, many hypocrites mingle with it, persons of immoral lives creep in, nay, many wicked men insinuate themselves; in consequence of which, numerous stains pollute that holy assembly, which Christ has separated for himself. . . .

So long as the pilgrimage of the Church in this world continues, bad men and hypocrites will mingle in it with those who are good and upright, that the children of God may be armed with patience, and, in the midst of offences which are fitted to disturb them, may preserve unbroken steadfastness of faith.

JOHN CALVIN

DO NOT BE SURPRISED

MATTHEW 13:27–28 ESV
*"And the servants of the master of the house came
and said to him, 'Master, did you not sow good
seed in your field? How then does it have weeds?'
He said to them, 'An enemy has done this.'"*

Now this Gospel teaches us how the kingdom of
God or Christianity fares in the world, especially
on account of its teaching, namely, that we are not to
think that only true Christians and the pure doctrine of
God are to dwell upon the earth; but that there must be
also false Christians and heretics in order that the true
Christians may be approved, as St. Paul says in 1 Corinthians 2:19. For this parable treats not of Christians, who are
so only outwardly in their lives, but of those who are
unchristian in their doctrine and faith under the name
Christian, who beautifully play the hypocrite and work
harm. It is a matter of the conscience and not of the hand.
And they must be very spiritual servants to be able to
identify the tares among the wheat. And the sum of all is
that we should not marvel nor be terrified if there spring
up among us many different false teachings and false
faiths. Satan is constantly among the children of God
(Job 1:6).

MARTIN LUTHER

HOW IS YOUR FRUIT?

MATTHEW 13:30 NIV
"'Let both grow together until the harvest.
At that time I will tell the harvesters: First collect
the weeds and tie them in bundles to be burned;
then gather the wheat and bring it into my barn.'"

God is sowing His Word in human hearts and looking for fruit ([Matthew 13] vv. 1–9, 18–23). He is sowing His people in the world where they can produce a harvest (vv. 24–30, 36–43). At the end of the age, He will separate the true from the false and the good from the bad.

Is your profession of Christ authentic? Or will you be seen as a counterfeit at the end of the age? (See Matthew 7:21–29).

Does your heart receive the Word? The seed has life and power and can produce a harvest of blessing in your life. Do you hear it?

Can God "plant you" where He wants you? You are a seed containing His divine life, but a seed must be planted to produce fruit (John 12:23–28).

Do you share with others what He teaches you (vv. 51–52)? Truth must not be hoarded; it must be shared so that others can be saved and built up in the faith.

WARREN W. WIERSBE

RISE UP IN FAITH

LUKE 13:18–19 ESV

He said therefore, "What is the kingdom of God like?
And to what shall I compare it? It is like a grain
of mustard seed that a man took and sowed in his
garden, and it grew and became a tree, and the
birds of the air made nests in its branches."

In these parables Christ encourages His disciples so that they may not shrink back in offence at the lowly beginnings of the Gospel. We see how irreligious men in their arrogance despise the Gospel, even laugh at it, because it is brought by obscure and unknown ministers, and because it is not received at once by universal applause, but has only a few followers and those mostly insignificant and mean. And so the weak come to despair of the outcome when they assess it by the beginnings. But it was deliberately that the Lord started His Kingdom from weak and lowly beginnings, so that the unlooked for progress might glorify His power the better. . . . Let us put up with the snarls and sneers of the proud until the Lord unexpectedly strikes them dumb. Meanwhile, let us not be cast down but let us rise up in faith against the contempt of the world until the Lord shows that incredible proof of His power which He proclaims here.

JOHN CALVIN

THE MUSTARD SEED

MATTHEW 13:31–32 NIV
*He told them another parable: "The kingdom
of heaven is like a mustard seed, which a man
took and planted in his field. Though it is the
smallest of all your seeds, yet when it grows, it is the
largest of garden plants and becomes a tree, so that
the birds of the air come and perch in its branches."*

The point of the parable is that this very little seed grows into a sizeable plant, one larger than all the plants of the garden, and indeed in its mature state becomes *a tree* (it can grow to a height of 8 to 12 feet). Jesus passes over the various stages of its growth; for this parable they are irrelevant. He is concerned with the contrast between the tiny seed and the mature majestic plant. . . . The kingdom may be considered insignificant in its beginnings and was doubtless despised by many in Jesus' day because of this. But in the end its growth would be extensive; it would be a very great kingdom indeed. There is also the thought of the continuity between the seed and the grown plant; it is from the mustard seed and that seed only that the mustard plant grew. So it is from Jesus and his little band that the mighty kingdom of heaven would emerge.

LEON MORRIS

THE MYSTERY OF GROWTH

MATTHEW 13:31–32 NRSV

He put before them another parable: "The kingdom
of heaven is like a mustard seed that someone took
and sowed in his field; it is the smallest of all the seeds,
but when it has grown it is the greatest of shrubs
and becomes a tree, so that the birds of the air
come and make nests in its branches."

Jesus does not compare the kingdom of God to a mustard seed but to *what happens* to a mustard seed. As God transforms a tiny speck of mustard seed into a six-to-ten-foot-high shrub . . . what God will accomplish through the death and resurrection of Jesus will be just as extraordinary. The tiniest of seeds grows into the greatest of shrubs, and how this happens is veiled in mystery. Even a modern scientific knowledge of the DNA structure of the mustard seed does not dispel the mystery of its growth. The seed holds within itself the power to transform itself dramatically into something else. One cannot make a judgment about its potential based on empirical evidence when it is in the seed stage. One could dismiss the microscopic seed as something inconsequential, but it has a power within itself to evolve into something that one cannot ignore and that eventually attracts the birds of heaven.

DAVID E. GARLAND

THE SEEDS AND THE SOIL

MATTHEW 13:2-3 NIV

Such large crowds gathered around him that he got into a boat and sat in it, while all the people stood on the shore. Then he told them many things in parables, saying: "A farmer went out to sow his seed."

It is not without good reason that the Evangelists begin with informing us that a vast multitude had assembled, and that when Christ beheld them, he was led to compare his doctrine to *seed*. That *multitude* had been collected from various places: all were held in suspense; all were alike eager to hear, but not equally desirous to receive instruction. The design of the parable was to inform them, that the *seed* of doctrine, which is scattered far and wide, is not everywhere productive; because it does not always find a fertile and well cultivated soil. Christ declared that he was there in the capacity of a husbandman, who was going out *to sow seed,* but that many of his hearers resembled an uncultivated and parched soil, while others resembled a thorny soil; so that the labour and the very seed were thrown away. . . . We need not wonder if, in our own day, the Gospel does not yield fruit in many.

JOHN CALVIN

PRAYER OF THE SEEDS

MARK 4:4–6 NLT

"As he scattered it across his field, some seed fell
on a footpath, and the birds came and ate it.
Other seed fell on shallow soil with underlying rock.
The plant sprang up quickly, but it soon wilted
beneath the hot sun and died because the roots
had no nourishment in the shallow soil."

Father, in the parable of the sower, You teach us that the seed of Your Word that falls along the path represents the ones who hear, and then the devil comes and takes away the word from their hearts, so that they may not believe (Luke 8:12). Lord, please help me to actively receive Your Word into my heart upon hearing it so that the devil cannot come and take it from me before it has had time to take root.

Father, I also pray that I will not be like those in the parable of the sower represented by the seed on the rock. They receive the word with joy when they hear it, but they have no root. They believe for a while, but in the time of testing they fall away (Luke 8:13). Help me to receive Your Word and hang on to it tightly when the time of testing comes.

BETH MOORE

CHOKING THORNS

MARK 4:7 ESV
"Other seed fell among thorns, and the thorns grew up and choked it, and it yielded no grain."

When Jesus told the parable of the soils (Mark 4:1–20), He said that some seed "fell among thorns, and the thorns came up and choked it." Then He interpreted the parable and said that the seed is the Word of God. The thorns choking the seed are "the worries of the world, and the deceitfulness of riches, and the desires for other things" (v. 19). Covetousness is the "desire for other things" in competition with the Word of God.

A real battle rages when the Word of God is preached. "The desire for other things" can be so strong that the beginnings of spiritual life can be choked out altogether. This is such a frightful warning that we should all be on our guard every time we hear the Word to receive it with faith and not choke it with covetousness. This is the conclusion of Jesus after telling that parable: "Therefore take care how you listen" (Luke 8:18).

JOHN PIPER

PREPARE YOURSELF FOR GOD'S WORD

MARK 4:20 NRSV

"And these are the ones sown on the good soil:
they hear the word and accept it and bear fruit,
thirty and sixty and a hundredfold."

Verse 20 says that good soil is the key to a fruitful hearing of the Word. I have said it several times before and no doubt will again: devote some time Saturday night and Sunday morning to prepare your heart for hearing the Word of God. The more you take time to humble yourself and purify your heart in prayer and tune the receiver of your mind into the wavelength of Christ, the more powerfully you will hear the Word and the more deeply you will worship.

I believe that if we as a church formed the habit of conscientiously preparing our hearts for hearing God's Word, the Lord might speak with such power that amazing changes would come into our lives for God's glory and for our joy. So let's resolve to take time for meditation and prayer and solitude and quiet walks in the snow, so that the soil of our heart is plowed deep for the Word of God.

JOHN PIPER

THE YEAST OF THE KINGDOM

LUKE 13:20–21 NLT
He also asked, "What else is the Kingdom of God like?
It is like yeast used by a woman making bread.
Even though she used a large amount of flour,
the yeast permeated every part of the dough."

In its present manifestation, the Kingdom of God is like a handful of leaven in a big bowl of dough. The dough swallows up the leaven so that one is hardly aware of its presence. It is almost unobservable; it can scarcely be seen. Instead of the glory of God shaking the earth, the Kingdom has come in One who is meek and lowly, who is destined to be put to death, who has only a handful of disciples. Little wonder that Roman historians hardly mention the career of Jesus. From the world's point of view, His person and mission could be ignored. But one should not be deceived thereby; some day the whole earth will be filled with God's Kingdom even as the leavened dough fills the entire bowl.

GEORGE ELDON LADD

THE FOLLY OF JUDGING

MATTHEW 13:33 NIV
He told them still another parable:
"The kingdom of heaven is like yeast that a
woman took and mixed into a large amount of
flour until it worked all through the dough."

This is a great tendency in men who suppose they have had some experience of the power of the Christian faith. They think they are able to discern and determine the state of others by a little conversation with them. Experience has taught me this is an error. There was a time when I did not imagine that the heart of man was so unsearchable as it is. I am less tolerant and less intolerant than once I was. I find more things in wicked men that may be counterfeit, even when they make a fair show of piety. I find more ways that the remaining corruption of the godly may make them appear like carnal men, formalists, and dead hypocrites than once I knew of. . . . We are so blind, full of pride, partial, prejudiced, and deceitful of heart. So He has committed it into the hands of One infinitely fitter for it and has made it His own right.

ARCHIE PARRISH AND R. C. SPROUL

GOD STARTS SMALL

MATTHEW 13:33 NLT
Jesus also used this illustration: "The Kingdom of Heaven is like yeast used by a woman making bread. Even though she used a large amount of flour, the yeast permeated every part of the dough."

The kingdom of God is nothing like the kingdom of the world. This was one of the central truths Jesus systematically instilled into the minds of his disciples. It functions on different principles with different purposes. The kingdom is ruled by love, not power, greed, or ambition.

Jesus called a few men to follow him and then spent three and one half years teaching and training them about the ways of God's kingdom. They entered the kingdom of God (John 3:3–8) when they responded to Jesus as lord in their lives. . . .

The world seeks to make big impressions with immediate results. God starts small. If God has the essence right, he will cause growth, small at first, unseen and unobserved (like yeast in bread). But in the end his rule will be extensive and thorough.

HENRY BLACKABY AND TOM BLACKABY

SILENCE

MATTHEW 13:33 ESV
*He told them another parable. "The kingdom of
heaven is like leaven that a woman took and hid
in three measures of flour, till it was all leavened."*

The kingdom of Christ is silent and imperceptible, like yeast. If the twin parable rebukes our cult of bigness, this story rebukes our cult of noise. Advertising does not help the church, unless it is as reverent as the gospel; and sensationalism can easily be a curse. The big booming forces soon pass: seed and leaven remain. The majestic power of the stars is silent, and the stars themselves are lowly as candles. Perhaps we need a "noise-abatement" movement in the church. Any true sound is born in silence.

But the kingdom, though silent, is yet dynamic. It is a yeasty ferment. It is a quiet revolution. No area of earth is left untouched by the redemptive trouble of its coming. The Epistle to Philemon is gentle enough and makes no noise, but it shows the yeast of the gospel subduing the stubborn dough of ancient slavery. In your heart and mine, and in the customs and institutions of our time, the leaven is at work.

GEORGE BUTTRICK

INVISIBLE INVADER

LUKE 13:20-21 NCV

Jesus said again, "What can I compare God's kingdom with? It is like yeast that a woman took and hid in a large tub of flour until it made all the dough rise."

One time Jesus likened his Kingdom to "yeast used by a woman making bread. Even though she used a large amount of flour, the yeast permeated every part of the dough" (Luke 13:21). Yeast suffuses the dough until the whole batch is leavened. Someone has said, "All silent forces are as all God's mightiest powers." Just as yeast is invisible when it has been kneaded into the dough and it becomes internal to the bread, so also, when the King of God's Kingdom enters our lives, he permeates and transforms us, subduing our hearts as yeast "subdues" the dough that it fills. . . .

Make very sure that, like yeast permeating a batch of dough, the Kingdom of Heaven is with you.

JILL BRISCOE

THE PRECIOUS PEARL

MATTHEW 13:45–46 NIV
*"Again, the kingdom of heaven is like a
merchant looking for fine pearls. When he
found one of great value, he went away and
sold everything he had and bought it."*

Again, the kingdom of heaven is said to be like a merchant who is seeking fine pearls. He finds one really precious pearl, and, having found it, he sells everything he has in order to buy it. In the same way, he who has a clear knowledge of the sweetness of heavenly life gladly leaves behind all the things he loved on earth. Compared with that pearl, everything else fades in value. He forsakes those things that he has and scatters those things that he has gathered. His heart yearns for heavenly things, and nothing on earth pleases him. The allure of earthly things has now dissipated, for only the brilliance of that precious pearl dazzles his mind. Solomon justly says of such love, "Love is strong as death," because just as death destroys the body, so ardent desire for eternal life cuts off the love for material things. For love makes insensitive to extraneous earthly desires the person whom it has swept off his feet.

GREGORY THE GREAT

THE SEEKING MIND

MATTHEW 13:45–46 NCV
*"Also, the kingdom of heaven is like a man looking
for fine pearls. When he found a very valuable pearl,
he went and sold everything he had and bought it."*

It was apparently by the sheerest chance that the man
found the hidden treasure; but it was at the end of a
long search that the merchant man found the pearl he had
been seeking all his life. So then, just as it is possible for a
man to discover the Kingdom almost accidentally, it is also
possible for him to arrive at it after a life-long search. . . .

There is a place in Christianity for the seeking mind.
"The unexamined life," said Plato, "is the life not worth
living." There is a duty on men to think things through.
Even if a man finds the Kingdom suddenly he is not
exempt from this duty; for he must still tease out the problem of what this means for him and for his life. No man
should be ashamed of his questionings and his doubts. So
many people's faith collapses when it meets with trouble
and sorrow and disaster simply because they have not
thought things out.

WILLIAM BARCLAY

THE PEARL OF GREAT PRICE

MATTHEW 13:45–46 ESV
"Again, the kingdom of heaven is like a merchant in search of fine pearls, who, on finding one pearl of great value, went and sold all that he had and bought it."

A tiny bit of sand lodges in the flesh of an oyster and becomes an irritating intrusion. Unable to expel it, the oyster covers the particle with layer after layer of a milky secretion until the irritation has become smooth, round, and acceptable. It also inadvertently becomes a precious gem.

An Oriental pastor once wrote, "Pearls, unlike other jewels, are drawn from the animate creation. (Other jewels are made from rocks and crystals and are mined out of the earth. . . .) Pearls are produced by life—a life which has overcome the working of death."

Jesus, the Pearl of great price, is unlike any other. . . . He is superior because his love poured forth from a life wounded by pain. He has become our example. We experience irritants in our lives, but God gives layer after layer of grace until the irritation becomes smooth and acceptable. What was an intrusion becomes a precious gem for all to admire . . . and for which God receives glory.

JONI EARECKSON TADA

THE NET

MATTHEW 13:47–48 ESV
*"Again, the kingdom of heaven is like a net
that was thrown into the sea and gathered
fish of every kind. When it was full, men
drew it ashore and sat down and sorted the
good into containers but threw away the bad."*

Again the kingdom of heaven is said to be like a fishing net that is let down into the sea, gathering all
kinds of fish. Once it is filled, the net is brought to shore.
The good fish are gathered into baskets, but the bad ones
are thrown away. Our holy church is compared to a net,
because it has been entrusted to fishermen, and because
all people are drawn up in it from the turbulent waters of
the present age to the eternal kingdom, lest we drown in
the depths of eternal death. This net gathers all kinds of
fish because it calls to forgiveness of sins everyone, wise
and foolish, free and slave, rich and poor, brave and weak.
Hence, the psalmist says to God: "Unto you shall all flesh
come." This net will be completely filled when it enfolds
the entire number of the human race at the end of time.

GREGORY THE GREAT

DRAWN INTO CHRIST

MATTHEW 13:47–48 NLT
*"Again, the Kingdom of Heaven is like a fishing
net that is thrown into the water and gathers fish
of every kind. When the net is full, they drag it
up onto the shore, sit down, sort the good fish
into crates, and throw the bad ones away."*

In the same way the Church exists for nothing else but
to draw men into Christ, to make them little Christs.
If they are not doing that, all the cathedrals, clergy, missions, sermons, even the Bible itself, are simply a waste of
time. God became Man for no other purpose. It is even
doubtful, you know, whether the whole universe was created for any other purpose. . . .

What we have been told is how we men can be drawn
into Christ—can become part of that wonderful present
which the young Prince of the universe wants to offer to
His Father—that present which is Himself and therefore
us in Him. It is the only thing we were made for. And
there are strange, exciting hints in the Bible that when we
are drawn in, a great many other things in Nature will
begin to come right. The bad dream will be over: it will
be morning.

C. S. LEWIS

THE MEANING OF THE KINGDOM

MATTHEW 13:47–48 NIV

*"Once again, the kingdom of heaven is like a net that
was let down into the lake and caught all kinds of fish.
When it was full, the fishermen pulled it up on
the shore. Then they sat down and collected the
good fish in baskets, but threw the bad away."*

By the Kingdom of Heaven sometimes is meant
Heaven and the state of happiness in another world;
here is meant the Christian Church, or the whole company of Christians all over the world.

The people of Christ are the Kingdom of Christ
because they are that part of the world that belongs to
Christ and that have Christ for their King. . . .

'Tis called the Kingdom of Heaven because Christ the
King is from Heaven . . . And the new heart and new
nature that his people have given them is holy and heavenly. And the country they are to live in forever, with
Christ their king, is Heaven.

'Tis said that this Kingdom of Heaven is like a net that
was cast into the sea. The sea is the whole world of
mankind. As a net that is cast into the sea [doesn't] take
all the fish in the sea, but only goes round and fences in a
few, so the Kingdom of Christ [doesn't] take all the world,
but only a part.

JONATHAN EDWARDS

FICKLE FOLLOWING

LUKE 9:61–62 NIV
Still another said, "I will follow you, Lord;
but first let me go back and say good-by
to my family." Jesus replied, "No one
who puts his hand to the plow and looks back
is fit for service in the kingdom of God."

And He raises the question in verse 62 about fickle following. The danger of indecisive discipleship. "No one, after putting his hand to the plow and looking back, is fit for the kingdom of God." You can't plow a straight furrow while looking back. You can't serve Christ, that is, you can't make Christ look great, if you are always second-guessing the value of following Him. . . .

But I want to close by saying, He is worthy! He is worth following, even through Jerusalem to the cross and to the nations. Yes, He will die in Jerusalem. But that is not bad news. Not anymore. That is our life. He loved us and gave Himself for us. . . . If you are with Him you will be saved, and not only will you be saved, you will be given a mission that according to verse 60 is more precious than burying your father. Namely, "Go and proclaim everywhere the kingdom of God in Christ Jesus."

JOHN PIPER

CONTINUE AND INCREASE

LUKE 9:62 NCV
*Jesus said, "Anyone who begins to
plow a field but keeps looking back is
of no use in the kingdom of God."*

Be careful that you don't pick up again anything you
once renounced and forsook. Beware that you don't
turn away from the field of evangelical work, contrary to
the Lord's command, and find yourself clothed in the coat
you once stripped off. Don't sink back to the world's low,
earthly lusts and desires. Don't defy Christ's word, come
down from the roof of perfection, and dare to take up
anything you have renounced and forsaken. Beware that
you don't remember your relationships or former affections, that you aren't called back to the cares and anxieties
of this world. . . . You should not only continue in this
humility and patience but also increase and go forward
with them. For although you should move on from the
early, beginning stages toward perfection, unfortunately
you begin falling back from these to even worse things. It
isn't those who begin these things who are saved, but
those who continue in them to the end.

JOHN CASSIAN

LET GO OF THE WORLD

LUKE 9:61–62 NRSV
*Another said, "I will follow you, Lord; but let me
first say farewell to those at my home." Jesus said
to him, "No one who puts a hand to the plow
and looks back is fit for the kingdom of God."*

The priority of discipleship is the same yesterday, today, and tomorrow: developing one's relationship to God. In order to avoid the errors that our instinct supplies to us, we must treat developing discipleship as a priority, understanding that the world will not comprehend when we go in a different direction from certain cultural expectations.

. . . The path to following Jesus is not a part-time job; it is a perpetual assignment. Since discipleship involves responding to people as well as to God, there is no moment when we are not "on call." Those who wish to pursue spirituality as a hobby will not discover its blessing. Jesus makes that truth clear by showing that even the highest commitments to family come in second place. We may be asked to go minister in places where our families may not be near. We may be asked to take risks for the sake of the gospel that no "sane" person might take. We may have to stand up for integrity in situations that might cost us dearly.

DARRELL L. BOCK

A TREASURE CHEST OF HOLY JOY

MATTHEW 13:44 NKJV

"Again, the kingdom of heaven is like treasure hidden in a field, which a man found and hid; and for joy over it he goes and sells all that he has and buys that field."

The kingdom of heaven is like treasure hidden in a field, which a man found and covered up; then from his joy he goes and sells all that he has and buys that field.

This parable describes how a person is converted and brought into the kingdom of heaven. He discovers a treasure and is impelled by joy to sell all he has in order to have this treasure. *You are converted to Christ when Christ becomes for you a treasure chest of holy joy.* The new birth of this holy affection is the common root of all the conditions of salvation. We are born again—converted—when Christ becomes a treasure in whom we find so much delight that trusting Him, obeying Him and turning from all that belittles Him becomes our normal habit. . . .

Without faith it is impossible to please God. For whoever would draw near to God must believe that He exists and *that He rewards those who seek Him.*

JOHN PIPER

WORTH SELLING EVERYTHING

MATTHEW 13:44 NASB
*"The kingdom of heaven is like a treasure hidden
in the field, which a man found and hid again;
and from joy over it he goes and sells all
that he has and buys that field."*

Jesus likens the kingdom to a man who finds *treasure . . . hidden in the field. Treasure* might denote the
place where valuables are kept . . . but here it is the valuable thing itself. In a day when places for keeping things
safe that we take for granted (like the safe deposit boxes in
banks) did not exist people had to make their own
arrangements. One method they employed was to bury
their valuable possessions (as did the unprofitable servant
who hid his talent . . .). If anyone did this before going
off on a journey and failed to return, the possessions
remained there and might be found later through a
chance discovery like that in this parable. . . . But acquir-
ing legal title to such a find was not always straightforward. . . . By buying the land before "lifting" the treasure,
he removed all possibility of dispute. . . . There can be
treasure, such that it is worth selling everything in order
to possess it. So with membership in the kingdom.

LEON MORRIS

THE GOSPEL IS A TREASURE

MATTHEW 13:45–46 NKJV
*"Again, the kingdom of heaven is like a
merchant seeking beautiful pearls, who,
when he had found one pearl of great price,
went and sold all that he had and bought it."*

The gospel too is a treasure, which was hidden in the
Old Testament, and then revealed when God gave
his Son. The Son he sacrificed was beyond price, so salvation cannot be purchased. Nothing will buy it and no
one can earn it. It is only granted as a free gift.

This short, stirring parable likens Christ to the precious
pearl, and we through faith may possess him. It is time to
reflect on the treasure that becomes ours when we receive
the gift of God, the treasure of life and truth, and know
for a certainty it is beyond price.

SARAH JEPSON COLEMAN

A PARABLE OF CONVERSION

MATTHEW 13:44 NCV

*"The kingdom of heaven is like a treasure hidden in
a field. One day a man found the treasure, and then
he hid it in the field again. He was so happy that he
went and sold everything he owned to buy that field."*

This parable describes how someone is converted and
brought into the kingdom of heaven. A person discovers a treasure and is impelled by joy to sell all that he
has in order to have this treasure. The kingdom of heaven
is the abode of the King. The longing to be there is not
the longing for heavenly real estate, but for camaraderie
with the King. The treasure in the field is the fellowship
of God in Christ.

I conclude from this parable that we must be deeply
converted in order to enter the kingdom of heaven and
that we are converted when Christ becomes for us a Treasure Chest of holy joy—a crucified and risen Savior who
pardons all our sins, provides all our righteousness, and
becomes in His own fellowship our greatest pleasure.

JOHN PIPER

THE HIGHEST PRIORITY

MATTHEW 13:44 NLT

*"The Kingdom of Heaven is like a treasure that
a man discovered hidden in a field. In his excitement,
he hid it again and sold everything he owned
to get enough money to buy the field—
and to get the treasure, too!"*

Jesus' point is that we must keep in check our own tendency to put the big things aside for the little ones. It's what Charles Hummel called the "tyranny of the urgent"—putting the more important thing behind the more immediate thing. At any given moment we need to be aware of the wisest possible way to invest the moment we so briefly hold in our grasp. Too easily a lifetime has passed and we've done little or nothing of eternal value. Stop to attend that funeral and you'll find five different reasons to change your mind about following Jesus; check in with your family and you're liable to be talked out of your new resolution. Jesus is simply making the point that a commitment to Him means a radical reprioritization of life's values—effective immediately.

. . . If you stumble across buried treasure, it will take precedence over everything else. You'll completely re-order the way you live (Matthew 13:44–46). Time is the ballot that records your vote on what matters in life.

DAVID JEREMIAH

BUY THE FIELD

MATTHEW 13:44 NRSV
*"The kingdom of heaven is like treasure hidden
in a field, which someone found and hid;
then in his joy he goes and sells all that
he has and buys that field."*

It's very much like the parable of the hidden treasure.
The key word in today's verse is [buy]. We must buy
the field. When we think of the field God wants us to
buy, we assume it's attractive, something we would love to
purchase anyway, a sun-drenched meadow dappled with
wildflowers. It rarely is. The field—that thing God wants
us to embrace—is usually bleak (like a sandlot with broken bottles and old tires scattered here and there). Of
course, once we know that the scrubby field contains a
treasure, the whole picture changes. The empty scrap of
land suddenly brims with possibility. Now we're ready to
sell everything to buy it. . . .

In my case, selling everything meant giving up self-pity
and resentment over a body that no longer worked. Selling everything meant tossing aside the questions and
investing the hours I sit in this wheelchair. It meant using
that time in God's Word and in prayer (the pick and
shovel needed to unearth the hidden treasure).

JONI EARECKSON TADA

A LIVING REALITY

MARK 1:15 NIV

"The time has come," he said. "The kingdom of God is near. Repent and believe the good news!"

Into this seething cauldron of popular expectation Jesus launched his dramatic announcement, 'The kingdom of God is near.' No wonder everyone stopped and took notice! Was the great moment of God's royal intervention, forecast so urgently by the Old Testament prophets, about to arrive?

It was. In fact, with Jesus' arrival on the world scene, it *had already come.* As Gabriel told Mary just before she became pregnant, 'The Lord God will give him the throne of his father David. His kingdom will never end.' God's kingdom is 'my kingdom,' Jesus told his followers later, and Paul does not feel at all awkward in writing about 'the kingdom of Christ and of God' (Ephesians 5:5).

In Jesus the kingdom of God had become a living reality. 'If I drive out demons by the finger of God,' he commented, 'then the kingdom of God has come to you.'

DAVID FIELD

THY KINGDOM COME

LUKE 11:2 NKJV
So He said to them, "When you pray, say:
Our Father in heaven, Hallowed be Your name.
Your kingdom come. Your will be done
On earth as it is in heaven."

The life of the planet, and especially its human life, is a life in which something has gone wrong, and badly wrong. Every time that we see an unhappy face, an unhealthy body, hear a bitter or despairing word, we are reminded of that. The occasional flashes of pure beauty, pure goodness, pure love, which show us what God wants and what he is, only throw into more vivid relief the horror of cruelty, greed, oppression, hatred, ugliness, and also the mere muddle and stupidity. . . . To say day by day "Thy Kingdom come"—if these tremendous words really stand for a conviction and desire—does not mean "I quite hope that some day the Kingdom of God will be established, and peace and goodwill prevail. But at present I don't see how it is to be managed or what I can do about it." On the contrary, it means, or should mean, "Here am I! Send me!"—active, costly collaboration with the Spirit in whom we believe.

EVELYN UNDERHILL

GRACE TO THE UNDESERVING

MATTHEW 9:12–13 NCV

When Jesus heard them, he said, "It is not the healthy people who need a doctor, but the sick. Go and learn what this means: 'I want kindness more than I want animal sacrifices.' I did not come to invite good people but to invite sinners."

This is a new departure in the relations of God and man; and new especially in that His grace is exhibited to the undeserving. "The Lord loveth the righteous, and His ear is open to their cry," said the old religion. But this is not now the whole story. To whom should the doctor come, if not to the sick? . . . So Jesus went about the towns and villages of Galilee, seeking the lost; and that was how the Kingdom of God came. He launched out into the deep, and all [the fish] came to His net. Nor was His appeal without results. The outcasts could be seen flocking into the Kingdom of God, as the birds fly to roost in the branches of a stalwart tree (which not long ago was an almost invisible seed). And for those who accepted the Kingdom of God there was pure happiness, like the joy of a wedding-feast.

C. H. DODD

THE FINAL OUTCOME

REVELATION 11:15 NKJV

Then the seventh angel sounded: And there were loud
voices in heaven, saying, "The kingdoms of this world
have become the kingdoms of our Lord and of
His Christ, and He shall reign forever and ever!"

There is also a 'now, but not yet' dimension to Jesus'
teaching about the kingdom of God. Although
God's rule is powerfully present in his own words and
actions, his stories-with-a-purpose (the parables) paint
word pictures of slow growth as the kingdom is gradu-
ally established, like yeast in dough or a small seed's
slow transformation into an impressive tree (see Matthew
13:31–33).

The final outcome, however, is inevitable. When Jesus
comes again to wind up the history of the world as we
know it, the kingdom of God will be displayed in total
triumph. Like it or not, all creation will submit to his
power. His royal status will be blazoned from one end of
the universe to the other. And he will emerge as his
church's great figurehead as it demonstrates 'the fullness of
him who fills everything in every way' (see Philippians
2:9–11; Matthew 24:30; Ephesians 1:22–23).

DAVID FIELD

PICTURES OF
FOLLOWING JESUS

———

*I consider everything a loss compared
to the surpassing greatness of knowing
Christ Jesus my Lord, for whose sake
I have lost all things. I consider them
rubbish, that I may gain Christ.*

PHILIPPIANS 3:8 NIV

PICTURES OF FOLLOWING JESUS

When Jesus asked people to follow Him, He expected a specific response. He heard answers like "maybe" and "later" as unacceptable forms of "no." As His parables made clear, Jesus taught that there are many ways to reject an invitation, but acceptance is a narrow response. The broad way is the wrong way, no matter how easy or good it looks. The right way will be tight, hard, and costly. Jesus wasn't joking when He said, "Just say a simple, 'Yes, I will,' or 'No, I won't.' Anything beyond this is from the evil one" (Matthew 5:37).

As you will find in the following readings, Jesus looked for a deliberate choice from His followers. He encouraged people to carefully count the cost, and then declare themselves. Apparently, an honest rejection that could later turn into a "yes" was more readily received than a lukewarm response (Revelation 3:15, 16). The following readings will help you clarify the way you are responding to God.

WALKING

LUKE 9:57–58 NIV
*As they were walking along the road, a man said to
him, "I will follow you wherever you go." Jesus replied,
"Foxes have holes and birds of the air have nests,
but the Son of Man has no place to lay his head."*

Christ himself was "in motion": he was not at home anywhere on earth, he was a wandering rabbi without a home, without the den of the foxes or the nest of the bird, without a cushion to rest his head, without ever having the prospect of returning to his own home. Nor was his food a solid, supratemporal truth-system, but the will of the Father at each instant. He walked in the light of this will, just as those who imitate him are to walk after him, that they may not walk in the darkness. . . .

"Walking" is a fundamental category of biblical and Christian existence: apart from walking, there is no certainty, no grasping of the truth, no standing fast. Christ himself fulfills the Old Testament attitude of walking before God, and he does this with all the mobility and flexibility of life that was expressed in this attitude. And only the one who walks remains related to Christ.

HANS URS VON BALTHASAR

DAY 56

THE SIN OF PRESUMPTION

LUKE 9:57–58 NLT

As they were walking along someone said to Jesus, "I will follow you no matter where you go." But Jesus replied, "Foxes have dens to live in, and birds have nests, but I, the Son of Man, have no home of my own, not even a place to lay my head."

The point is that, in this life and in the world to come, those who follow Jesus will receive everything they want, if what they want is to follow Jesus. If, on the other hand, following Jesus is not what they want, then . . . there is no point in following Jesus. Living in the way, the truth, and the life is—for those who know Christ as the way, the truth and the life—self-evidently preferable to the alternative, which is being lost, ignorant, and dead. . . . Those who presume to think that they and others of like religious doctrine, experience, or way of life are the first and will therefore be both the first and the last in line for salvation have not, one fears, understood the generosity of the Lord of the vineyard. Nor do they take as seriously as we all should the sin of presumption.

RICHARD JOHN NEUHAUS

THE HIDING PLACE

LUKE 9:57–58 NASB

*As they were going along the road, someone said
to Him, "I will follow You wherever You go."
And Jesus said to him, "The foxes have holes
and the birds of the air have nests, but the
Son of Man has nowhere to lay His head."*

O Lord Jesus Christ, the birds have their nests, the
foxes their holes, and Thou didst not have whereon
to lay Thy head. Homeless wert Thou upon earth, and
yet a hiding-place, the only one, where a sinner could
flee. And so today Thou art still the hiding-place; when
the sinner flees to Thee, hides himself in Thee, is hidden
in Thee— then he is eternally defended, then "love" hides
a multitude of sins.

PERRY D. LEFEVRE

THE CALL TO SUFFER

LUKE 9:58 ESV
*And Jesus said to him, "Foxes have holes,
and birds of the air have nests, but the Son
of Man has nowhere to lay his head."*

The first disciple offers to follow Jesus without waiting to be called. Jesus damps his ardour by warning
him that he does not know what he is doing. In fact he
is quite incapable of knowing. That is the meaning of
Jesus' answer—he shows the would-be disciple what life
with him involves. We hear the words of One who is on
his way to the cross, whose whole life is summed up in
the Apostles' Creed by the word "suffered." No man can
choose such a life for himself. No man can call himself to
such a destiny, says Jesus, and his word stays unanswered.
The gulf between a voluntary offer to follow and genuine
discipleship is clear.

DIETRICH BONHOEFFER

JESUS ABOVE ALL ELSE

LUKE 9:59 NIV
He said to another man, "Follow me."
But the man replied, "Lord, first
let me go and bury my father."

Jesus [tests] you . . . to see if this is enough, to see if He is really your treasure, your joy, your security, your hope, your friend in times of loneliness, your home, your father and mother, your power to look straight ahead—to test you in all these ways, He tells you what it will cost.

. . . The point of all these tough words as Jesus interacts with different people is not to create laws that all disciples or all missionaries have to keep: Thou shalt give all your money! Thou shalt give half your money! Thou shalt go without a bed! Thou shalt go without a funeral for your dad! The point is that Jesus knows everyone's idol. . . .

Don't take offense. He does this to win us for Himself. "Follow me!" is the goal. Being with Jesus is the goal. It won't be easy. But it will be good.

JOHN PIPER

STRONGER THAN OUR BARRIERS

LUKE 9:59–60 NASB

And He said to another, "Follow Me."
But he said, "Lord, permit me first to go and bury
my father." But He said to him, "Allow the
dead to bury their own dead; but as for you,
go and proclaim everywhere the kingdom of God."

But where Jesus calls, he bridges the widest gulf. The second would-be disciple wants to bury his father before he starts to follow. He is held bound by the trammels of the law. He knows what he wants and what he must do. Let him first fulfil the law, and then let him follow. A definite legal ordinance acts as a barrier between Jesus and the man he has called. But the call of Jesus is stronger than the barrier. At this critical moment nothing on earth, however sacred, must be allowed to come between Jesus and the man he has called—not even the law itself. Now, if never before, the law must be broken for the sake of Jesus; it forfeits all its rights if it acts as a barrier to discipleship. Therefore Jesus emerges at this point as the opponent of the law, and commands a man to follow him. Only the Christ can speak in this fashion. He alone has the last word.

DIETRICH BONHOEFFER

DIVINE APPOINTMENTS

LUKE 9:59–60 NLT
The man agreed, but he said, "Lord, first let me
return home and bury my father." Jesus replied,
"Let those who are spiritually dead care for their
own dead. Your duty is to go and preach
the coming of the Kingdom of God."

I believe that sometimes God gives us explicit instructions for the moment before us. I know He does for me. I don't hear voices, but in the midst of all my busyness and distractions the still, small voice breaks through: Why don't you call this particular friend? Why don't you go to that particular place? I think it's common in the life of ministers. Sometimes I obey what I know to be the voice of God. Other times, to my shame, I let the moment get by; I tell God, in essence, "Let me go bury the dead first." And I know deep down that I've missed a divine appointment. It's an empty feeling to comprehend, much later, that you've missed something special God had for you to do.

We need to hear His voice, particularly as it pertains to the immediate use of our time. If we could do that, even moderately well, the fruit of our lives would be orchards ample enough to feed the world.

DAVID JEREMIAH

GOD'S PURPOSES

LUKE 9:59 NCV
Jesus said to another man, "Follow me!"
But he said, "Lord, first let me go
and bury my father."

No master has so many servants as our Master; and for each He has a suitable employment. Even the little maid was at hand to testify to Naaman in his need. Many of us murmur against the position God has given us. We want to do this, but God puts us into that. We have an ambition to serve Him here, but His plan for us lies elsewhere. When faced by such apparent reverses, it is well to remember that God's purpose for us goes back before our conversion, for His foreknowledge has determined our circumstances even before we were born. God never does a thing suddenly; He has always prepared long, long before. So there is nothing to murmur about, nothing to be proud of, in the calling of God. There is also no one of whom to be jealous, for other people's advantages have nothing to do with us. When we look back over life, we bow and acknowledge that all was prepared by God.

WATCHMAN NEE

DAY 63

WHAT IT MEANS TO LOVE JESUS

MATTHEW 16:24–26 ESV
*Then Jesus told his disciples, "If anyone would
come after me, let him deny himself and take up
his cross and follow me. For whoever would save
his life will lose it, but whoever loses his life for
my sake will find it. For what will it profit a man
if he gains the whole world and forfeits his life?
Or what shall a man give in return for his life?"*

Blessed is he who understandeth what it is to love
Jesus, and to despise himself for the sake of Jesus. We
must leave what is beloved, for the sake of the Beloved;
for Jesus will be loved alone and above all things. The love
of things created is deceitful and inconstant; the love of
Jesus is faithful and enduring. He that clingeth to the
creature shall fall with its falling. He that embraceth Jesus
shall be firmly rooted forever. Love Him, and keep Him
for thy friend, who, when all forsake, will not leave thee,
nor suffer thee to perish finally. . . . In life and in death
keep thyself near to Jesus, and entrust thyself to His
fidelity, who alone can help thee when all others fail.

THOMAS À KEMPIS

LOSE YOUR LIFE TO KEEP IT

MATTHEW 16:25 NLT
*"If you try to keep your life for yourself,
you will lose it. But if you give up your
life for me, you will find true life."*

My dear friend, the more you can leave yourself behind, the more you will be able to enter into me. Just as longing for nothing outside of yourself makes for inner peace, so does letting go of yourself unite you with God. I want you to learn to abandon yourself perfectly to my will, without grumbling or complaining. . . .

If you wish to enter into life, keep the commandments. If you wish to know the truth, believe in me. If you wish to be perfect, sell all that you have. If you wish to be my follower, deny your very self. If you wish to have a blessed life, see this present life for what it is. If you wish to be exalted in heaven, humble yourself in this world. If you wish to reign with me, carry my cross, for only the servants of the cross find the road of blessedness and true light.

THOMAS À KEMPIS

A LIVING SACRIFICE

ROMANS 12:1 ESV

*I appeal to you therefore, brothers, by the mercies
of God, to present your bodies as a living sacrifice,
holy and acceptable to God, which is
your spiritual worship.*

With my hands outstretched on the cross and my body naked, I freely offered myself to God the Father for your sins. Nothing was left in me that was not given to God. In the very same way—with all your strength and love—you too should willingly offer yourself to me. . . .

What more do I ask of you than yourself? I do not care at all for anything else that you may give me. I do not seek your gift. I seek you. Just as it would not satisfy you to have anything but me, so it does not please me to have anything you may give, if you do not give yourself. . . .

I have said this, and I mean it: "Unless a person renounces all that he has, he cannot be my follower." So, if you wish to be my disciple, give yourself to me with your whole heart.

THOMAS À KEMPIS

TOTAL COMMITMENT

MATTHEW 10:38-39 NCV

*"Whoever is not willing to carry the cross and follow
me is not worthy of me. Those who try to hold on to
their lives will give up true life. Those who give up
their lives for me will hold on to true life."*

This kind of total commitment can sound very frightening because it costs us everything. But look at the payoff! Jesus did not come into the world to overpower us or deprive us, he came to empower us and to bless us abundantly. As he said: "I came so that they might have life and have it more abundantly" (John 10:10).

The prideful desire to determine our own destiny can only produce sin which, as we know, brings forth death. Obedience, on the other hand, brings forth life. As Paul said to the Romans, ". . . just as through the disobedience of one person the many were made sinners, so through the obedience of one the many will be made righteous" (Romans 5:19). That one man, of course, is Christ. . . . Christ was God's expression of love to the world. Obedience, therefore, becomes the result of our love response to God and cannot be based on power, domination, legalities, or manipulation.

JOHN MICHAEL TALBOT

DAY 67

SHARING THE CUP OF SUFFERING

ROMANS 8:17 NRSV
*. . . and if children, then heirs, heirs of God and joint
heirs with Christ—if, in fact, we suffer with him
so that we may also be glorified with him.*

Lord God almighty, Father of your dear and blessed
Son Jesus Christ, through whom we have been
granted to know you; you are God over all. . . .

I thank you today for the privilege of being counted
among those who have witnessed to you with their lives;
of sharing the cup of suffering which Christ drank; and of
rising again to life everlasting with him, in body and soul,
and in the immortality of the Holy Spirit.

May I be received today into your presence, a costly
sacrifice and so an acceptable one. This is all part of your
plan and purpose, and you are now bringing it to pass. For
you are the God of truth, and in you is no falsehood
at all.

For this, and for all the other things you have done for
me, I bless and glorify you, through our eternal high
priest in heaven, your dear Son, Jesus Christ, who shares
with you and the Holy Spirit glory for ever. Amen.

POLYCARP

HIS YOKE IS LIGHT

1 JOHN 5:3 NKJV
For this is the love of God,
that we keep His commandments.
And His commandments are not burdensome.

For nothing is grievous or burdensome to him who loves. They are not grievous, because love makes them light; they are not grievous, because Christ gives strength to bear them. Wings are no weight to the bird, which they lift up in the air until it is lost in the sky above us, and we see it no more, and hear only its note of thanks. God's commands are no weight to the soul which, through His Spirit, He up-bears to himself; nay, rather, the soul, through them, the more soars aloft and loses itself in the love of God. "The commandments of God are not grievous," because we have a power implanted in us mightier than all which would dispute the sway of God's commandments and God's love, a power which would lift us above all hindrances, carry us over all temptations, impel our listlessness, sweep with it whatever opposes it, sweep with it even the dulness or sluggishness of our own wills—the almighty power of the grace of God.

EDWARD B. PUSEY

BE PREPARED

LUKE 14:28–29 NLT

"But don't begin until you count the cost. For who would begin construction of a building without first getting estimates and then checking to see if there is enough money to pay the bills? Otherwise, you might complete only the foundation before running out of funds. And then how everyone would laugh at you!"

The gospel implies that those who try to build a tower, but spend all their time on the foundation and never finish, are ridiculous. From the Parable of the Tower, we also learn to work hard and finish every lofty goal, to complete the work of God through the varied structures of His commandments. Of course, one stone doesn't make an entire tower any more than obeying one commandment lifts the soul to the required height of perfection. By all means, the foundation must be laid first. But, as the Apostle Paul says, the structure of gold and precious gems must be built over it.

GREGORY OF NYSSA

COUNT THE COST

LUKE 14:28 NCV
*"If you want to build a tower, you first sit down
and decide how much it will cost, to see if
you have enough money to finish the job."*

It often turns out, that many succumb to the slightest test, because they imagined to themselves a state of pure delight, as if they would forever be in the shelter, or a life of ease. No one will ever be a fit soldier of Christ who does not equip himself, a long time before, for the campaign. The similes focus on this point very sharply. Building is a business full of labour and frustration, and in terms of costs far from satisfying. As for war (which involves so many upsets, in fact virtually threatens to destroy the human race) no one starts this unless by compulsion. Yet the very convenience of having a house induces men to have no hesitation in pouring out their substance, while necessity also forces us to spare no expense in waging wars. But the prize that awaits the builders of the temple of God, and the recruits to Christ's army, is of far greater excellence.

JOHN CALVIN

REPENTANCE

LUKE 14:28–30 NIV
*"Suppose one of you wants to build a tower.
Will he not first sit down and estimate the cost
to see if he has enough money to complete it?
For if he lays the foundation and is not able
to finish it, everyone who sees it will ridicule
him, saying, 'This fellow began to build and
was not able to finish.'"*

At times Jesus appeared to discourage potential disciples from following him (cf. Matt. 8:18–20); what he was discouraging was not following him but following him without "counting the cost." The kingdom of God is offered graciously by God to all. Exclusion from it is due not to the difficulty of "earning" entrance but rather to the willful rejection of the gracious invitation (cf. here Luke 14:15–24). Yet the grace of God is not "cheap grace." It is grace pure and simple, but it is a commitment to the rule of grace in one's life. One can only receive the grace of God with open hands, and to open those hands one must let go of all that would frustrate the reception of that grace. Jesus refers to this letting go as repentance. In our parables he told his audience that they should consider what this repentance involved before they received the grace of the kingdom.

ROBERT H. STEIN

FIX YOUR EYES ON JESUS

LUKE 14:31–33 NIV

*"Or suppose a king is about to go to war against
another king. Will he not first sit down and consider
whether he is able with ten thousand men to oppose
the one coming against him with twenty thousand?
If he is not able, he will send a delegation while the
other is still a long way off and will ask for terms
of peace. In the same way, any of you who does not
give up everything he has cannot be my disciple."*

Will your Christian life be only half built and then
abandoned because you did not count the cost of
commitment to Jesus? What are those costs? Christians
may face loss of social status or wealth. They may have to
give up control over their money, their time, or their
career. They may be hated, separated from their family,
and even put to death. Following Christ does not mean a
trouble-free life. We must carefully count the cost of
becoming Christ's disciples so that we will know what we
are getting into and won't be tempted later to turn back.

LIFE APPLICATION BIBLE

THE HARD TRUTH

LUKE 14:33 ESV

*"So therefore, any one of you who does not
renounce all that he has cannot be my disciple."*

Taking our stand on biblical truth can be our only
defense against our culture's penchant to reduce all
issues to simplistic suppositions and glib answers. We im-
patiently expect to get solutions to the most profound
ambiguities of life the same way we drive up to the fast-
food counter. . . .

The problem is, that "easy-answer" mentality is invad-
ing the Christian church: we want scorecards by which
we can instantly rate our politicians, new catchy acronyms
for salvation, time-saving techniques for discipleship. . . .

In our well-intentioned effort to reach unsaved masses,
we often make the gospel message itself sound easy,
unthreatening, a painless answer to all life's ills. We portray a loving God who forgives all and asks nothing in
return. . . .

As citizens in the holy nation, we must challenge pre-
suppositions—not only of society as a whole but of the
evangelical subculture as well. The Gospel of Jesus Christ
must be the bad news of the conviction of sin before it
can be the good news of redemption.

CHARLES COLSON

Following Christ Today

Luke 14:33 NIV

"In the same way, any of you who does not give up everything he has cannot be my disciple."

When Jesus walked among humankind there was a certain simplicity to being a disciple. Primarily it meant to go with him, in an attitude of study, obedience, and imitation. There were no correspondence courses. One knew what to do and what it would cost. . . .

Of course, attitudes that define the disciple cannot be realized today by leaving family and business to accompany Jesus on his travels about the countryside. But discipleship can be made concrete by loving our enemies, blessing those who curse us, walking the second mile with an oppressor—in general, living out the gracious inward transformations of faith, hope, and love. Such acts—carried out by the disciplined person with manifest grace, peace, and joy—make discipleship no less tangible and shocking today than were those desertions of long ago. Anyone who will enter into The Way can verify this, and he or she will prove that discipleship is far from dreadful.

DALLAS WILLARD

ENTHUSIASM FOR CHRIST

LUKE 14:33 NKJV
*"So likewise, whoever of you does not forsake
all that he has cannot be My disciple."*

If you want to know what Jesus taught, know Him. . . .
You have but to turn and gaze upon His countenance,
behold His actions, and note His spirit, and you know His
teaching. He lived what He taught.

If we wish to know Him, we may hear His gentle voice
saying, "Come and see." Study His wounds, and you understand His innermost philosophy. "To know Him and
the power of His resurrection" (Philippians 3:10) is the
highest degree of spiritual learning. . . .

If people have enthusiastically loved Christianity, it is
because first of all they loved Christ. For Him apostles
labored, and for Him confessors were brave. For Him
saints have suffered the loss of all things, and for Him mar-
tyrs have died. The power that creates heroic consecration
is Jesus Christ Himself. The memories stirred by His
name have more influence over hearts than all things in
earth or heaven. The enthusiasm that is the life of our
holy cause comes from Himself.

C. H. SPURGEON

DENIAL OF SELF

PHILIPPIANS 3:8 ESV

*Indeed, I count everything as loss because of the
surpassing worth of knowing Christ Jesus my Lord.
For his sake I have suffered the loss of all things and
count them as rubbish, in order that I may gain Christ.*

Those who have not denied themselves cannot follow
Jesus. For choosing to follow Jesus and to actually
follow Him springs from no ordinary courage. Those
who deny themselves wipe out their former, wicked lives.
For example, those who once were immoral deny their
immoral selves and become self-controlled forever. . . .
Those who have become righteous don't confess themselves but Christ. Those who find wisdom, because they
possess wisdom, also confess Christ. And those who,
"with the heart believe unto righteousness, and with the
mouth make confession unto salvation," and testify for
Christ's works by confessing them to others, will be con-
fessed by Christ before His Father in heaven. . . . As a
result, let every thought, every purpose, every word, and
every action become a denial of ourselves and a testimony
about Christ and in Christ. I am persuaded that the perfect person's every action is a testimony to Christ Jesus
and that abstinence from every sin is a denial of self, leading to Christ. Those people are crucified with Christ.

ORIGEN

CLINGING TO THE CROSS

HEBREWS 12:2 NKJV
*. . . looking unto Jesus, the author and finisher
of our faith, who for the joy that was set before Him
endured the cross, despising the shame, and has sat
down at the right hand of the throne of God.*

The Christian life involves hard work. It requires us to give up whatever endangers our relationship with God, to run patiently, and to struggle against sin with the power of the Holy Spirit. To live effectively, we must keep our eyes on Jesus. We will stumble if we look away from him to stare at ourselves or at the circumstances surrounding us. We should be running for Christ, not ourselves, and we must always keep him in sight.

LIFE APPLICATION BIBLE

OUR FIRST LOVE

REVELATION 2:4 NIV
*"Yet I hold this against you:
You have forsaken your first love."*

Ever to be remembered is that best and brightest of hours, when first we saw the Lord, lost our burden, received the roll of promise, rejoiced in full salvation, and went on our way in peace. . . . We rejoiced with thanksgiving; we magnified the holy name of our forgiving God, and our resolve was, "Lord, I am thine, wholly thine; all I am, and all I have, I would devote to thee. Thou hast bought me with thy blood—let me spend myself and be spent in thy service. In life and in death let me be consecrated to thee." How have we kept this resolve? Our espousal love burned with a holy flame of devoutedness to Jesus—is it the same now? Might not Jesus well say to us, "I have somewhat against thee, because thou hast left thy first love"? Alas! it is but little we have done for our Master's glory. . . . O quicken us that we may return to our first love, and do our first works!

C. H. SPURGEON

BUILDING ON THE FOUNDATION

1 CORINTHIANS 3:11 NASB
*For no man can lay a foundation other than
the one which is laid, which is Jesus Christ.*

We are given a foundation of excellence, truth, justice, service, sharing, and unselfish love. How should we build on this foundation? I can think of five ways, all admirable. One is good living, based on prayer and constant communication with God. A second is holiness, a life in which we are careful to avoid sin. A third is the spirit-filled, or charismatic, life, exemplified by the disciples at Pentecost. Another is to be compassionate to the poor, perhaps building houses for them. And a final one is evangelism, telling people about Jesus Christ.

. . . Harmony can be reached by referring to the most exalted goals of Christianity. It seems illogical, but these are the ones that require the most modest talents, intelligence, and influence. When we remember the pure teachings of Jesus, we realize that any human being can espouse truth, justice, humility, and compassion. This is where we find the common foundation for our Christian lives.

JIMMY CARTER

SINCERITY

MARK 10:21–22 NRSV
Jesus, looking at him, loved him and said,
"You lack one thing; go, sell what you own, and
give the money to the poor, and you will have
treasure in heaven; then come, follow me."
When he heard this, he was shocked and went
away grieving, for he had many possessions.

I suppose, the rich young man we read of (Mark 10:17–22) might have what is called moral sincerity. But he had no sincerity in the covenant of grace. When he came to Christ to know what he should do to have eternal life, 'tis probable he ignorantly thought himself willing to yield himself to Christ's direction. Yet when it came to a trial, and Christ told him he must go and sell all that he had, and give to the poor, it proved that he had no sincerity of willingness at all for any such thing. So that it is evident, however unsanctified men may be morally sincere in some things, yet they have no sincerity of any sort in that covenant, of which the sacraments are seals; and that moral sincerity, distinct from gracious, in this covenant, is a mere imagination, there being indeed no such thing.

JONATHAN EDWARDS

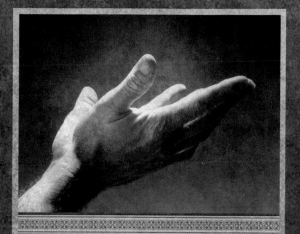

PICTURES OF
SERVICE AND
OBEDIENCE

*"If you love me,
you will obey what I command."*
JOHN 14:15 NIV

PICTURES OF SERVICE
AND OBEDIENCE

Jesus looked for eyes that saw and ears that heard. He noticed people who put faith to action. He confronted those who pretended to be one thing when they were truly just the opposite. His stories made sense, but uncommon sense. And they stung those among His listeners who identified with the villains in the parables.

Those who live by the rules of the kingdom of God turn away from the demand for fairness. They hunger and thirst for righteousness. They recognize that life isn't fair, and the greatest example of unfairness is God's overwhelming grace toward them.

Many of Jesus' parables call into question our fondest expectations and desires. They remind us that those who base their lives on Christ can still experience storms and wind, difficulties and disappointments. Those who truly follow Christ don't do so because of the rewards but because they see no other way or One to follow. Note the sharp edge of truth Jesus conveys in the following parables.

GOD'S FREEDOM

MATTHEW 20:1–4 NRSV

*"For the kingdom of heaven is like a landowner
who went out early in the morning to hire laborers
for his vineyard. After agreeing with the laborers
for the usual daily wage, he sent them into his
vineyard. When he went out about nine o'clock,
he saw others standing idle in the marketplace; and
he said to them, 'You also go into the vineyard, and
I will pay you whatever is right.' So they went."*

Jesus told a parable about a landowner who hired a series
of workers. No matter at what point in the day he
added the workers, at the end, "Each of them received
the usual daily wage" (Matthew 20:9). The others, some
of whom had labored from early in the morning, were
furious when Jesus showed that God is free to forgive
whom he wants to forgive. That God is not bound by the
regulations made up by our own limited expectations.

HENRI NOUWEN

LATE ARRIVALS

MATTHEW 20:9–10 KJV
*And when they came that were hired about
the eleventh hour, they received every man a
penny. But when the first came, they supposed
that they should have received more; and
they likewise received every man a penny.*

The parable contains a warning to those who . . .
might feel that they deserve more for their faithfulness than the late arrivals. He deals with this problem very
directly in the Parable of the Prodigal Son. The brother
who had never left his father envies the lavish welcome
the wayward son receives on his return. The early history
of the Church provides an example of a late arrival in the
Apostle Paul, who had persecuted the Church. Those
who had been with the Lord from the beginning found
no little difficulty in accepting this new apostle as their
equal, but the grace of God proved more powerful than
any supposedly normal human inclination. . . .

Envy has no place in the kingdom. Those who are
"first" may become last or even be excluded if they are
filled with pride, resentment, and selfishness. God wills
that all should be saved and come to the knowledge of the
truth (1 Timothy 2:4). His servants ought to be of the
same mind.

ARCHBISHOP DMITRI

ARE YOU ENVIOUS?

MATTHEW 20:15 NIV
*"Don't I have the right to do what I want with
my own money? Or are you envious
because I am generous?"*

When I was a child (as now) there were stories I found difficult, such as that of the workers in the vineyard, where those who had worked only an hour were paid as much as those who had worked all day in the heat of the sun. It wasn't fair! Like most children, I wanted things to be fair, even though life had already taught me that unfairness abounds. I think many of us still feel like the child stamping and crying out, "It's not fair!" Those who have worked all day long should certainly be paid more than those who came in at the last minute! But Jesus is constantly trying to make us understand that God's ways are not our ways, and that God's love is far less selective and far greater than ours. "Is thine eye evil because I am good?" God asks in Matthew's Gospel after he has finished paying all the workers the same wage. When God blesses those we deem unworthy, does our jealousy make our eye become evil?

MADELEINE L'ENGLE

GOD'S GENEROSITY

MATTHEW 20:15–16 NRSV

"'Am I not allowed to do what I choose with what
belongs to me? Or are you envious because
I am generous?' So the last will be first,
and the first will be last."

The parable is all to do with the master's generosity. But the parable is preceded by the enigmatic saying: 'Many who are first will be last, and many who are last will be first' (Matthew 19:30), and is followed by the almost identical saying: 'So the last will be first, and the first last' (20:16). These sayings make it clear that the parable is not just about the master's generosity, but about the surprising upside-down effects of that generosity. . . .

For the rich and the religious such egalitarian salvation did not always seem good news, since it meant giving up their present advantage and special position. The rich man accordingly went away sad, and in the parable those who had worked all day complained of the master's unfair generosity. But for those in need of employment at the eleventh hour the master's generosity was good news indeed, and for the sinners whom he welcomed into his company Jesus and his revolution were wonderful good news.

DAVID WENHAM

TRUE GIVING

MATTHEW 6:1, 3 NIV
*"Be careful not to do your 'acts of righteousness'
before men, to be seen by them. If you do,
you will have no reward from your Father
in heaven. . . . Do not let your left hand know
what your right hand is doing."*

Such sincere almsgiving is not to be found among worldly people; their contributing is the kind that gives with the right hand and grasps with the left hand. . . . They want to buy you for a trifle and to hold you as their perpetual prisoner—your body and your life and everything you have—along with God Himself. For that reason Christ says: "When you are giving alms with your right hand, be careful that you do not try to take more with your left hand. Hold it behind your back, and do not let it know anything about what is going on." Then you may be said to be "contributing with single-ness," not to be taking or to be giving in such a way as to make the other person owe you ten times as much as you gave him, or to make him celebrate and adore you as an idol. . . . My friend, if you can sell your trifles for such a price, you are really quite a salesman!

MARTIN LUTHER

HOW TO BE HUMBLE

MATTHEW 6:3–4 NASB

*"But when you give to the poor, do not let your left
hand know what your right hand is doing,
that your giving may be in secret; and your Father
who sees what is done in secret will reward you."*

Nurture a love to do good things in secret, concealed
from the eyes of others, and therefore not highly
esteemed because of them. Be content to go without
praise, never being troubled when someone has slighted
or undervalued you. . . .

When you do receive praise for something you have
done, take it indifferently and return it to God: Reflect it
back to God, the giver of the gift, the blesser of the action,
the aid of the project. Always give God thanks for making you an instrument of his glory for the benefit of
others.

. . . Make a good name for yourself by being a person
of virtue and humility. It is a benefit for others who hear
of you to hear good things about you. As a model, they
can use your humility to their advantage. . . . Be like
Moses, whose face shined brightly for others to see but
did not make it a looking glass for himself.

JEREMY TAYLOR

HIDDEN WORKS

MATTHEW 6:3–4 NRSV

"But when you give alms, do not let your
left hand know what your right hand is doing,
so that your alms may be done in secret; and
your Father who sees in secret will reward you."

Y es," says the Spirit, "that they may rest from their
labors; and their works do follow them." And then
there shall be rest from our labors, that is, from the strain
and the sin and the temptations that we stand under
today; there shall be no more fear of growing weak, no
fear of sin and of the force of Babylon; then there shall be
rest, because we shall see and recognize Christ as the
Lord. "And their works do follow them"—they do not
pave the way for us to Christ, for faith does that—but
they follow, the works that are done in God, in Christ, for
which he prepared us from the very beginning of the
world; we don't recognize them here; they are hidden;
they are the works about which the left hand knows not
what the right hand does. But they shall be with us,
because they belong to us as the everlasting gift of God.

DIETRICH BONHOEFFER

LIVING FOR GOD

MATTHEW 6:4 ESV

*". . . so that your giving may be in secret. And your
Father who sees in secret will reward you."*

Some people are surprised at Christ's teaching about
rewards; they think it makes the Christian life sound
mercenary. But we must not be super-spiritual about this;
Jesus wouldn't! The reward motive is powerful, and he
appeals to it. To understand his mind, however, we must
remember that the rewards belong within the context of
the family relationship between Christians and their heavenly Father.

Parents often reward children for doing things they
ought to be doing anyway. They love to encourage and
help the child. The reward comes as a gift, not a merit-
badge. . . .

The activity of which Matthew chapter 6 speaks is the
service of God: looking toward him, reaching out to him,
praising, praying, worshipping, adoring, loving, and obeying him, and thus enjoying fellowship with him. . . . Our
reward will be that for which we have been qualifying
throughout our discipleship on earth: God's welcome, his
"well done!" and the communication to us of his love in
his immediate actual presence.

J. I. PACKER

LEAVE SOMETHING BEHIND

1 CORINTHIANS 3:9 NRSV
For we are God's servants, working together;
you are God's field, God's building.

U p and *be doing,"* is the word that comes from God
for each of us. Leave some "good work" behind
you that shall not be wholly lost when you have passed
away. Do something worth living for, worth dying for. Is
there no want, no suffering, no sorrow that you can
relieve? Is there no act of tardy justice, no deed of cheerful kindness, no long-forgotten duty that you can perform? Is there no reconciliation of some ancient quarrel,
no payment of some long-outstanding debt, no courtesy,
or love, or honor to be rendered to those to whom it has
long been due; no charitable, humble, kind, useful deed
by which you can promote the glory of God, or good
will among men, or peace upon earth? If there be any
such deed, in God's name, in Christ's name, go and do it.

ARTHUR P. STANLEY

WHOLE-HEARTED OBEDIENCE

EZEKIEL 36:27 ESV
*And I will put my Spirit within you, and
cause you to walk in my statutes and
be careful to obey my rules.*

He sees whether I have indeed chosen and given myself up to the whole-hearted performance of every known command. He sees whether I am really longing and learning to know and do all His will. And when His child does this, in simple faith and love, the obedience is acceptable. The Spirit gives us the sweet assurance that we are well-pleasing to Him, and enables us to 'have confidence before God, because we know that we keep His commandments, and do the things that are pleasing in His sight.'

This obedience is indeed an attainable degree of grace. The faith that it is, is indispensable to the obedient walk.

You ask for the ground of that faith in God's Word? You find it in God's New Covenant promise,

'I will write My law in their heart. I will put My fear in their heart, and they shall not depart from Me.'

ANDREW MURRAY

KEEP DOING YOUR JOB

MATTHEW 25:14–15 NRSV

"For it is as if a man, going on a journey, summoned his slaves and entrusted his property to them; to one he gave five talents, to another two, to another one, to each according to his ability. Then he went away."

Now you've got the picture. The landowner went away and gave his three servants some specific things to administrate. He rode off down the road on his donkey and disappeared into the distance. Now . . . what must those servants do? They must discipline themselves to continue acting and doing business just as if the master were still with them.

It isn't easy to stay accountable when the boss isn't looking over your shoulder, is it? It isn't easy to keep the routine when you don't have to get up at the specific time or punch a time clock. In this case, the boss couldn't check in by cell phone, . . . text messaging, or e-mail. The servants are simply left to do their work; he has to trust them to act in his best interest. As usual, two servants responded one way, and one responded in another way.

DAVID JEREMIAH

THE GIFT OF THE SPIRIT

MATTHEW 25:15 NASB
*"To one he gave five talents, to another, two,
and to another, one, each according to his
own ability; and he went on his journey."*

Jesus' parable of the talents recorded in Matthew 25:14–30 was a warning that it is possible for us to misjudge our capacities. This parable has nothing to do with natural gifts and abilities, but relates to the gift of the Holy Spirit as He was first given at Pentecost. We must never measure our spiritual capacity on the basis of our education or our intellect; our capacity in spiritual things is measured on the basis of the promises of God. If we get less than God wants us to have, we will falsely accuse Him as the servant falsely accused his master when he said, "You expect more of me than you gave me the power to do. You demand too much of me, and I cannot stand true to you here where you have placed me." When it is a question of God's Almighty Spirit, never say, "I can't."

OSWALD CHAMBERS

INVEST IN THE FUTURE

MATTHEW 25:16–18 NIV

*"The man who had received the five talents went at
once and put his money to work and gained five more.
So also, the one with the two talents gained two more.
But the man who had received the one talent went off,
dug a hole in the ground and hid his master's money."*

This is a parable of capitalism, a parable of productiv-
ity. Jesus is saying with respect to stewardship, as well
as service, that His people are called to delay their gratification. We are called to invest in the future so that our
investments may grow. He tells this story of the rich master who has to go away, just as Jesus has ascended into
heaven and left us behind with the treasures that we have
during His absence. . . . We may be "unprofitable," but
that doesn't mean we're to be unproductive. "Let's sleep
in tomorrow, hide our gifts, so that when He comes back,
we can say, 'Here are the gifts You gave us. Nothing happened to them. They're just as good as when you left.'"
Jesus says, "I'll take that away from you and give it to the
man who multiplied his gifts ten times, who used the gifts
I gave him for the sake of the kingdom."

R. C. SPROUL

GOD IS THE OWNER

MATTHEW 25:19–21 NCV

*"After a long time the master came home and asked
the servants what they did with his money. The servant
who was given five bags of gold brought five more bags
to the master and said, 'Master, you trusted me to care
for five bags of gold, so I used your five bags to earn
five more.' The master answered, 'You did well. You
are a good and loyal servant. Because you were loyal
with small things, I will let you care for much greater
things. Come and share my joy with me.'"*

When the Possessor of heaven and earth brought
you into being, and placed you in this world, he
placed you here, not as a proprietor, but a steward: As such
he entrusted you, for a season, with goods of various
kinds; but the sole property of these still rests in him, nor
can ever be alienated from him. As you yourself are not
your own, but his, such is, likewise, all that you enjoy.
Such is your soul and your body, not your own, but
God's. And so is your substance in particular. And he has
told you, in the most clear and express terms, how you are
to employ it for him, in such a manner, that it may be all
a holy sacrifice, acceptable through Jesus Christ. And this
light, easy service, he hath promised to reward with an
eternal weight of glory.

JOHN WESLEY

DON'T HIDE YOUR TALENTS

MATTHEW 25:20–21 NIV
*"The man who had received the five talents brought
the other five. 'Master,' he said, 'you entrusted me
with five talents. See, I have gained five more.'*
*"His master replied, 'Well done, good and faithful
servant! You have been faithful with a few things;
I will put you in charge of many things.'"*

I long to say truthfully of you, "Lord, Thou gavest me
five talents, behold I have gained five other talents."
Then, I could show the precious talents of your righteousness! "For we have a treasure in earthen vessels."
These are the talents which the Lord begs us to trade with
spiritually: the two coins of the New and the Old Testament that the Samaritan left for the robbed man to get his
wounds healed. . . . Therefore, we must not keep the
Lord's money buried and hidden in the flesh. Don't hide
your one talent in a napkin, but like a good business-
person, always work with your mind, body, and a steady,
ready will to distribute it. Then the Word will be near
you, in your mouth and heart. The Word of the Lord is
the precious talent that redeems you. Such money must
often be seen on people's tables so that, by constantly trad-
ing the good coins, they can go into every land and purchase eternal life.

AMBROSE

KEEP WORKING

MATTHEW 25:22–23 NLT

"Next came the servant who had received the two bags of gold, with the report, 'Sir, you gave me two bags of gold to invest, and I have doubled the amount.' The master said, 'Well done, my good and faithful servant. You have been faithful . . . Let's celebrate together!'"

One of the criticisms often leveled at those who believe in the Rapture and imminent return of Jesus Christ is that such beliefs lead to a life of laziness and indolence.

After all, we know He is coming back. We know the end of the story. We've read the last chapter in the Book. Why should we entangle ourselves in the messy affairs of this passing world? . . .

In direct contrast to that attitude, in a story told in the Book of Luke, Jesus used a phrase that keeps ringing in my ears. In my heart, I believe it ought to be the watchword for all believers who long for His coming: "Do business till I come." I love that. . . .

The parable of the talents teaches us what to do while we are waiting. The bottom line? We need to be working. We're not to be sitting around drinking diet soda and playing Bible Monopoly. We're to be involved, energized, doing business for our Lord.

DAVID JEREMIAH

LET YOUR LIGHT SHINE

MATTHEW 25:25–26 NASB

*"'And I was afraid, and went away and hid
your talent in the ground. See, you have what
is yours.' But his master answered and said
to him, 'You wicked, lazy slave.'"*

In our Lord's parable of the talents, the 'good and faithful' servants were those who furthered their master's interests by making the most enterprising lawful use that they could of what was entrusted to them. The servant who buried his talent, and did nothing with it beyond keeping it intact, no doubt imagined that he was being extremely good and faithful, but his master judged him to be 'wicked,' 'slothful,' and 'unprofitable.' For what Christ has given us to use must be put to use; it is not enough simply to hide it away. We may apply this to our stewardship of the gospel. The truth about salvation has been made known to us, not for us simply to preserve (though we must certainly do that), but also, and primarily, for us to spread. The light is not meant to be hidden under the bushel. It is meant to shine; and it is our business to see that it shines.

J. I. PACKER

THE DANGER OF DOING NOTHING

MATTHEW 25:26–27, 30 ESV
*"But his master answered him, 'You wicked and
slothful servant! . . . You ought to have invested
my money with the bankers, and at my coming
I should have received what was my own with
interest. . . . And cast the worthless servant
into the outer darkness. In that place there
will be weeping and gnashing of teeth.'"*

What this parable teaches is the same thing Paul
taught, namely, that there are varying degrees of
reward for the faithfulness of our lives. But it also moves
beyond that and teaches that there is a loss not only of
reward, but of heaven, for those who claim to be faithful
but do nothing to show that they prize God's gifts and
love the Giver. That's the point of the third servant who
did nothing with his gift. He did not just lose his reward,
he lost his life. Jesus says in Matthew 25:30, "Cast out the
worthless slave into the outer darkness; in that place there
shall be weeping and gnashing of teeth."

. . . Salvation is shown by deeds. So when Paul says (in
2 Corinthians 5:10) that each "[will] be recompensed . . .
according to what he has done," he not only means that
our rewards will accord with our deeds, but also our salvation will accord with our deeds.

JOHN PIPER

DON'T PLAY IT SAFE

MATTHEW 25:28–29 ESV

*"So take the talent from him and give it to
him who has the ten talents. For to everyone
who has will more be given, and he will have
an abundance. But from the one who has not,
even what he has will be taken away."*

Then, as hearers of the parable, we wait for the punch line we think we see coming. The benefactor will say, "Play it safe like the one talent man. Don't play the ponies. God is a hard God. Treasure what he gives you so you'll be sure you still have it the next time he checks you out." Only of course that's just what the benefactor doesn't say, as Jesus tells it. It is the all-or-nothing ones who are held up as shining examples of what it is to have faith, to have life, to have courage or whatever it is it takes, and the better-be-safe-than-be-sorry one who gets it in the neck for taking the faith or life or courage or whatever it is he's been given and tucking it under his tail and sitting on it like an old grad on a hot water bottle at the fifty-yard line on a chilly October Saturday.

FREDERICK BUECHNER

A PURE HEART

PSALM 24:3–4 ESV
Who shall ascend the hill of the LORD?
And who shall stand in his holy place?
He who has clean hands and a pure heart,
who does not lift up his soul to what is false
and does not swear deceitfully.

In the case of some who have despised the greatest possessions of this world, and not only large sums of gold
and silver but also large properties, we have seen them
afterwards disturbed and excited over a knife or pencil or
pin or pen. . . . They are without the love of which the
apostle speaks: *"If I give away all my possessions, and if I hand
over my body so that I may boast, but do not have love, I gain
nothing."* And from this it clearly follows that perfection is
not arrived at simply by self-denial. . . . That love consists
in purity of heart alone. For not to be *envious or boastful or
arrogant or rude,* not to *insist on* one's *own way,* not to *rejoice
in wrongdoing,* not to think evil, and so on—what is all this
except always to offer to God a perfect and clean heart
and to keep it free from all disturbances?

JOHN CASSIAN

CHRIST IS THE ROCK

MATTHEW 7:24–25 ESV

"Everyone then who hears these words of mine and does them will be like a wise man who built his house on the rock. And the rain fell, and the floods came, and the winds blew and beat on that house, but it did not fall, because it had been founded on the rock."

For, unless a man acts upon what he hears or perceives, he does not fix it firmly. So, if Christ is the rock (as many testimonies of the Scriptures proclaim), then a man builds on Christ if he acts upon what he hears from Christ. *'The rain fell, the floods came, the winds blew and beat against that house; but it did not fall, because it was founded on a rock.'* So that man fears neither the fog of superstition (for what else is understood by the word, '*rain*,' when it is used in the sense of something bad?), nor the murmurings of men (for I think that these are compared with the winds), nor the flux of this life (which floods the earth, as it were, with carnal lusts). Whoever dwells beneath the pleasing promises of those three things is crushed by their calamities. But, if a man has his house founded on a rock, he fears none of those things.

AUGUSTINE

BUILD ON THE ROCK

MATTHEW 7:24 NLT
*"Anyone who listens to my teaching
and obeys me is wise, like a person
who builds a house on solid rock."*

As with the faith of the disciples, we should speak frequently with our Master. For the world is like the sea to us, beloved. We sail on this sea, with our own free will acting like the wind. For we all navigate according to our will. If the Word is our pilot, we enter into rest. But if pleasure takes hold of us, we face the danger of storms and are shipwrecked. . . . "When affliction or persecution ariseth, the unbeliever is offended," the Lord said. Because unbelievers aren't strengthened by the faith and because they favor temporal things, they can't stand up against difficulties. Like the foolish man's house built on sand, those without understanding fall under storms of temptation. The saints, however, have exercised their senses to be self-controlled. . . . They wake up the Lord who is with them and are delivered. Because they find relief as they pass through water and fire, they celebrate by offering up thankful prayers to God who has rescued them.

ATHANASIUS

THE ONLY SAFE FOUNDATION

MATTHEW 7:24–25 NKJV

*"Therefore whoever hears these sayings of Mine, and
does them, I will liken him to a wise man who built his
house on the rock: and the rain descended, the floods
came, and the winds blew and beat on that house;
and it did not fall, for it was founded on the rock."*

In this parable Jesus is making a staggering claim. In
effect He is saying that obedience to His teaching is the
only safe foundation for life. He is saying that unless a
man takes Him as master he cannot look for anything else
but the ruin of his life. In anyone else a claim like that
would be regarded as megalomaniac egotism. Other teachers make appeals, give advice, offer counsel; but Jesus
presents men with an imperious demand. . . .

[Lord Nelson was a gentlemanly captain in his day.] It
is told that Nelson was famous for his courtesy to defeated
enemies. On one occasion a defeated captain came on to
Nelson's quarterdeck as a prisoner. He had heard of Nelson's courtesy and he came forward holding out his hand
almost as if he were at a reception. Nelson spoke one sentence. "Your sword first," he said, "and then your hand."
The first necessity was submission. This parable teaches
clearly that the claim of Christ must either be totally
accepted or totally rejected.

WILLIAM BARCLAY

OUR ONLY REFUGE

MATTHEW 7:24–25 NASB

*"Therefore everyone who hears these words of Mine
and acts upon them, may be compared to a wise man
who built his house upon the rock. And the rain fell,
and the floods came, and the winds blew and
slammed against that house; and yet it did not fall,
for it had been founded on the rock."*

Perhaps you've seen the film *Lawrence of Arabia*. The
real T. E. Lawrence, who was a secret agent during
the First World War, often engaged in desert guerrilla
warfare against the Turks. The enemy forces who chased
Lawrence constantly often felt they had him hemmed in
and trapped. But he would ride to his hidden desert
fortress. He was never too far away from it, and if worse
came to worst, he could flee there, find safety, and
strengthen himself on the ample provisions of food and
water. Lawrence had a refuge, a rock, and a fortress in the
dangers of the wilderness. But God provides a much better
one for you and me.

In those times when we feel the hostile forces of the
world pursuing us, we long for a strong refuge. As we feel
suddenly exposed and vulnerable and our feet are unsteady
in the shifting sands beneath us, we yearn for a rock and
a fortress—the kind of security found only in God.

DAVID JEREMIAH

PUT THEM INTO PRACTICE

MATTHEW 7:26–27 NIV

*"But everyone who hears these words of mine and
does not put them into practice is like a foolish man
who built his house on sand. The rain came down,
the streams rose, and the winds blew and beat
against that house, and it fell with a great crash."*

Every day we are training ourselves in one direction or
the other by the thoughts we think, the words we say,
the actions we take, the deeds we do. This sense of pro-
gression in character, in either one direction or the other,
is also taught in Romans 6:19. Paul refers to the Roman
Christians' former bondage to sin and to *ever-increasing
wickedness*. They were well on their way to becoming
experts in wickedness. But now, says Paul, having been
freed from the slavery of sin, they are to offer their bodies in slavery to righteousness *leading to holiness*. Righteousness refers here to obedience to God, specific "right
actions." Holiness refers to the state or character resulting
from those actions; right actions, or obedience, leads to
holiness. Of course, both the actions and the character are
the result of the working of the Holy Spirit, but he works
as we work, and we are able to work because he is at work
in us.

JERRY BRIDGES

WOLVES IN SHEEP'S CLOTHING

MATTHEW 7:15 NIV

"Watch out for false prophets. They come to you in sheep's clothing, but inwardly they are ferocious wolves."

Look how He describes the outward appearance and impression of the false teachers. In the first place, He gives them the name "prophets;" that is what they are called, and that is what they are, teachers and preachers. They boast of the fact that they have no other title or reputation than this, that they have the very same office of the ministry, the same Scriptures, and the same God as the others. Nevertheless they are false prophets. . . .

In the second place, He says that they come in sheep's clothing, that they are irreproachable and outwardly indistinguishable from genuine preachers. . . . Who is there among the common people that can oppose these men or dare to denounce them? Who even knows how to protect himself against them, since they claim to come with the name and the Word of God?

MARTIN LUTHER

PEARLS BEFORE SWINE

MATTHEW 7:6 NLT

"Don't give what is holy to unholy people.
Don't give pearls to swine! They will trample
the pearls, then turn and attack you."

When Jesus sent the seventy disciples out to proclaim the gospel, he told them to travel light. He
told them that when they came to a village, if the people
refused to hear them, they were to shake the dust off their
feet and go elsewhere. It's in that kind of a context that
Jesus talked about giving pearls to swine. In reaching out
to others with the gospel, we're not to give up easily (this
patient attitude runs through several parables and in Scripture in general). But from the standpoint of strategy,
it's ineffective to be reaching out constantly to people
who are steadfastly, adamantly opposed to the Christian
faith. . . .

If people despise the things of God, we are certainly not
supposed to write them off or to stop being concerned
about them, but at the same time, we're not supposed to
invest our best things over and over again in those people.

R. C. SPROUL

REFUSING TO DIE

JOHN 12:24 NCV
*"I tell you the truth, a grain of wheat must fall
to the ground and die to make many seeds. But if
it never dies, it remains only a single seed."*

I f it die . . ." What is this death? It is the cracking open
of the shell by the working of temperature and humid-
ity, so that the true life within the grain can express itself.
It is all too possible for a Christian to have the Lord's life
in him and yet for that life to be confined and suppressed
by the hard shell of nature. So we have the sad fact of a
fruitless Christian. In this case it is not a matter of obtain-
ing life, for that came at conversion, but of the release of
that life so that it can grow and be fruitful.

If we wrap ourselves in our natural shell and resist
Christ's call to share his cross and be broken open, we will
hinder the possibility of God-glorifying fruit. We may
enjoy some inward blessing ourselves, but it is only when
that inner life is dispersed around us that others can benefit from our lives.

WATCHMAN NEE

EXAMINE YOURSELF

MATTHEW 7:18–19 NIV
*"A healthy tree cannot bear bad fruit,
nor can a diseased tree bear good fruit.
Every tree that does not bear good fruit
is cut down and thrown into the fire."*

The self-examination which the Scriptures enjoin (in 1 Corinthians 11:28, for example), is not for the purpose of finding something within to make me more acceptable to God, nor as a ground of my justification before Him; but is with the object of discovering whether Christ is being formed in me. There are two extremes to be guarded against: such an undue occupation with the work of the Spirit within, that the heart is taken off from the work of Christ for His people; and, such a one-sided emphasis upon the imputed righteousness of Christ that the righteousness imparted by the Spirit is ignored and disparaged. It is impossible that the Third Person of the Trinity should take up His abode within a soul, without effecting a radical change within him: and it is this which I need to make sure of. It is the Spirit's work within the heart which is the only infallible proof of salvation.

A. W. PINK

WANTING TO DO GOD'S WILL

PHILIPPIANS 2:13 NASB
. . . for it is God who is at work in you,
both to will and to work for
His good pleasure.

I t is altogether the way we look at things, whether we think they are crosses or not. And I am ashamed to think that any Christian should ever put on a long face and shed tears over doing a thing for Christ which a worldly person would be only too glad to do for money.

What we need in the Christian life is to get believers to *want* to do God's will as much as other people want to do their own will. And this is the idea of the Gospel. It is what God intended for us; and it is what He promised. In describing the new covenant in Hebrews 8:6–13, He says it shall no more be the old covenant made on Sinai, that is, a law given from the outside, controlling a man by force—but it shall be a law written *within,* constraining us by love.

HANNAH WHITALL SMITH

LAYING UP TREASURE IN HEAVEN

MATTHEW 6:20–21 NLT

*"Store your treasures in heaven, where they will
never become moth-eaten or rusty and where they
will be safe from thieves. Wherever your treasure is,
there your heart and thoughts will also be."*

To lay up treasure in heaven is to do arts which promote, or belong to, the kingdom of God; and what
our Lord assures us of is that any act of our hands, any
thought of our heart, any word of our lips, which pro-
motes the divine kingdom by the ordering whether of
our own life or of the world outside—all such activity,
though it may seem for the moment to be lost, is really
stored up in the divine treasure-house; and when the
heavenly city, the New Jerusalem, shall at last appear, that
honest effort of ours, which seemed so ineffectual, shall be
found to be a brick built into that eternal and celestial
fabric.

CHARLES GORE

RECEIVING THE NEW LIFE

1 PETER 1:13 NIV
Therefore, prepare your minds for action;
be self-controlled; set your hope fully on the grace
to be given you when Jesus Christ is revealed.

That is why the real problem of the Christian life comes where people do not usually look for it. It comes the very moment you wake up each morning. All your wishes and hopes for the day rush at you like wild animals. And the first job each morning consists simply in shoving them all back; in listening to that other voice, taking that other point of view, letting that other larger, stronger, quieter life come flowing in. And so on, all day. . . .

We can only do it for moments at first. But from those moments the new sort of life will be spreading through our system: because now we are letting Him work at the right part of us. . . . When He said, "Be perfect," He meant it. He meant that we must go in for the full treatment. It is hard; but the sort of compromise we are all hankering after is harder—in fact, it is impossible.

C. S. LEWIS

PICTURES OF
LOVING OUR
NEIGHBORS

*"My command is this: Love each other
as I have loved you."*

JOHN 15:12 NIV

PICTURES OF LOVING
OUR NEIGHBORS

Obedience doesn't automatically follow understanding. We don't have to worry about the difficulty and cost of loving our neighbor if we can endlessly argue about the identity of our neighbor. We can superficially agree that loving others is good but keep our actual lack of love hidden under the cover of intentional confusion. Even the apparently loving act of offering to remove a sliver from someone's eye becomes suspect if it is merely a diversion from the grotesque stake clouding our vision.

Although we make many choices in life, Jesus pointed out that we don't get to choose our neighbors. We only get to choose whether or not we are going to love them as we ought. In the company of those who love Jesus, we will continually be surprised over who turns out to love us unexpectedly. Good Samaritans are not only worth imitating; they are worth appreciating. Meet some of them in the pages of this section.

BLESS THOSE WHO CURSE YOU

LUKE 6:28 ESV
*"Bless those who curse you,
pray for those who abuse you."*

Beloved, how should we regard the loving-kindness of our Savior? We should cry out and praise His goodness with power and with trumpets! Not only should we appear like Him, but should follow Christ's example for heavenly conversation. We should carry on what He began. In suffering, we shouldn't threaten. When we are verbally abused, we shouldn't berate in return. Instead, we should bless those that curse us and commit ourselves to God in everything. For He judges righteously. Those who do this adapt themselves to the gospel. They will have a part with Christ, and, as imitators of apostolic conversation, He considers them worthy of praise. They will receive the praise Paul gave to the Corinthians when he said, "I praise you that in everything ye are mindful of me." Afterwards, because some people perverted Paul's words . . . he proceeded to say, "And as I have delivered to you traditions, hold them fast." Of course that means that we shouldn't think things other than what the Teacher has delivered.

ATHANASIUS

A NEW COMMAND

JOHN 13:34–35 NIV
*"A new command I give you: Love one another.
As I have loved you, so you must love one another."*

The Master held himself before the disciples as an example to emulate: "As I have loved you, so you must love one another." But the challenge is so great and the consequences so far-reaching, that there is always a tendency for us to treat such a statement with benign neglect, as if to say tacitly, "It is truly a wonderful concept, and the world would be a better place if it worked. But it won't work. It's just too much!" I offer two responses to this reaction.

First, Jesus . . . said, "A new *command* I give you: Love one another" (John 13:34, italics added). A commandment is not a suggestion!

Second, this teaching was given about the time Jesus introduced the disciples to the ministry of the Holy Spirit. Among other things, . . . it meant dependence upon the Holy Spirit to work in them continually, because they would always find themselves inadequate. It is only through obedience and dependence that the capacity to love as commanded becomes even a remote possibility.

JILL AND STUART BRISCOE

THE SPECK AND THE PLANK

MATTHEW 7:3–4 NIV

*"Why do you look at the speck of sawdust in your
brother's eye and pay no attention to the plank in
your own eye? How can you say to your brother,
'Let me take the speck out of your eye,' when all
the time there is a plank in your own eye?"*

Lord, I must ask myself why I look at the speck of sawdust in another person's eye and pay no attention to
the plank in my own eye. How can I say to my brother,
"Let me take the speck out of your eye," when all the
time there is a plank in my own eye? O God, rescue me
from being a hypocrite! Give me the honesty and courage
to first take the plank out of my own eye, and then I may
see clearly to remove the speck from another person's eye
(Matthew 7:3–5).

BETH MOORE

JUDGING OTHERS

MATTHEW 7:4 NKJV

*"Or how can you say to your brother,
'Let me remove the speck from your eye';
and look, a plank is in your own eye?"*

Is Jesus telling us not to evaluate and assess others at all? No. It's human nature to form judgments; we might not share our private evaluation of people and events, but we can't avoid using our evaluative faculties.

Jesus is not telling us to deny our humanity and stop using our minds in this way. But he is warning us against a particular pitfall by pointing out that we should judge ourselves by the standards which we bring to the judgment of others.

We must expect God to judge us as we judge others; so, if we want him to judge us compassionately, we had better judge others compassionately. Also, we need to make sure that our judgment of others is preceded by honest judgment of ourselves before the Lord on those matters for which we criticize others. So often we compensate for our own uneasiness in some area by coming down heavily on someone else for failing in that same area.

J. I. PACKER

HYPOCRISY

MATTHEW 7:5 NIV
"You hypocrite, first take the plank out of your own eye, and then you will see clearly to remove the speck from your brother's eye."

In other words, first rid yourself of hatred, and then you will immediately be able to correct the man you love. The word, *'hypocrite,'* is aptly employed here, since the denouncing of evils is a matter for upright men of good will. When evil men engage in it, they impersonate others; like masqueraders, they hide their real selves beneath a mask, while they portray another's character through the mask. . . . Therefore, whenever necessity compels us to reprove or rebuke someone, we ought to proceed with piety and caution. First of all, let us consider whether the man's fault is such as we ourselves have never had, or whether it is one that we have overcome. Then, if we have never had such a fault, let us remember that we are human, and could have had it. But, if we have had it and are rid of it now, let us remember our common frailty, in order that mercy—and not hatred—may lead us to the giving of reproval or rebuke.

AUGUSTINE

REMOVE THE PLANK

MATTHEW 7:4-5 NRSV

*"Or how can you say to your brother, 'Let me take
the speck out of your eye,' while the log is in
your own eye? You hypocrite, first take the log
out of your own eye, and then you will see clearly
to take the speck out of your neighbor's eye."*

For the verdict that one's brother needs a splinter taken
from his eye does not come from concern but from
contempt for humanity. Even while one is putting on a
mask of love toward others, one is actually performing a
deed of consummate evil by inflicting numerous criticisms and accusations on close companions, thereby
usurping the rank of teacher when one is not even worthy to be a disciple. For this reason he called this one
"hypocrite."

. . . You see that Jesus does not forbid judging but commands that one first remove the plank from one's own
eye. One may then set right the issues relating to others.
For each person knows his own affairs better than *others*
know them. And each one sees major faults easier than
smaller ones. And each one loves oneself more than one's
neighbor. So if you are really motivated by genuine concern, I urge you to show this concern for yourself first,
because your own sin is both more certain and greater.

JOHN CHRYSOSTOM

GENTLE CORRECTION

GALATIANS 6:1 NASB

*Brethren, even if anyone is caught in any trespass,
you who are spiritual, restore such a one in a
spirit of gentleness; each one looking to yourself,
so that you too will not be tempted.*

W hen Jesus said, "Judge not, that you not be judged," he did not mean that we were not to be concerned about our own and other people's faults. What he was against was a censorious, fault-finding spirit which gets malicious pleasure from pointing out other people's failings. . . .

This is very different from what Paul calls for here: gently and humbly drawing a fellow Christian's attention to something that needs to be put right in his life and actually helping him to do that, aware all the time of our own weaknesses. . . .

Jesus was marvelously creative in his relationships. He never said more at any stage than the other person was able to hear; sometimes he gave enigmatic answers to their first questions so that they could think their way into what he was saying and then be able to ask better questions and thus take matters further. Love gave him fantastic empathy with others. We need love like that.

J. I. PACKER

LOVE AND PRAYER

LUKE 10:27 NIV

*He answered: "'Love the Lord your God with
all your heart and with all your soul and with
all your strength and with all your mind';
and, 'Love your neighbor as yourself.'"*

God's love demands expression; it cannot stand alone. It is how God "breathes," if you will. Just as our blood *must* flow from our heart to our lungs, so God's love *must* flow out to his creation. Therefore, if we love God with all our heart, soul, mind, and strength, we will be drawn of necessity to our neighbor. . . . It is only through the royal law of love that our deeds of mercy and compassion become a blessing. Without it, try as we might to do otherwise, our serving will always be tinged with condescending arrogance. . . .

Prayer makes our love flow freely, both vertically and horizontally. As we pray, we are drawn into the love of God, which irresistibly leads us to our neighbor. When we try to love our neighbor, we discover our utter inability to do so, which irresistibly drives us back to God. And so we enter into that never-ending fellowship of love that gives Christian community its life.

RICHARD J. FOSTER

WHO IS MY NEIGHBOR?

LUKE 10:28–30 NKJV

And He said to him, "You have answered rightly;
do this and you will live." But he, wanting to justify
himself, said to Jesus, "And who is my neighbor?"
Then Jesus answered and said: "A certain man
went down from Jerusalem to Jericho . . ."

Some people try to escape [the Ten Commandments']
force by limiting the definition of neighbor. But
when Jesus was asked, "Who is my neighbor?" He told
the parable of the good Samaritan, which teaches that
every person we meet is our neighbor (Luke 10:29–37).
No man anywhere, no matter who he is or what he is
like, no matter what language he speaks, what skin color
he has, or what social or cultural group he belongs to, is
excluded from being my neighbor. This is an absolute
standard which we must practice, not just a vague emotional reaction. If we do not practice this, we are sinning
and will be judged.

FRANCIS A. SCHAEFFER

OUR NEED FOR EACH OTHER

LUKE 10:30 NASB

*Jesus replied and said, "A man was going
down from Jerusalem to Jericho, and fell
among robbers, and they stripped him and beat
him, and went away leaving him half dead."*

The reality of it is more than that. As we travel around
this world, every man that we meet is the man in the
ditch because every man that we meet, no matter how little he looks it and no matter how surprised he might be
to realize it, is half dying for need of us—not just of the
next person who comes along, though of him too, but of
us. In one way or another, every human being is crying
out or acting out, or at great cost stifling his need to
be known, accepted, forgiven, and healed by us, of all
people. . . .

There seems then to be a deeper and more terrible
truth still, because to be really alive, not just half alive, we
need to help and heal him: his need for mercy is matched
by our need to be merciful. It is not just for his sake that
we come to his rescue. It is also for our sakes.

FREDERICK BUECHNER

REASON AND CHARITY

Now by chance a certain priest came down that road.
And when he saw him, he passed by on the other side.

B e just and equitable in all your actions. . . . Always
put yourself in your neighbor's place and him in
yours, and then you will judge rightly. Imagine yourself
the seller when you buy and the buyer when you sell and
you will sell and buy justly. All these injustices are slight
and do not oblige us to restitution since we abide solely
by rigorous terms that are in our favor. Yet we are obliged
to make amendment since they are great faults against
reason and charity. In the end they are simply acts of
self-deceit, for a man loses nothing by living generously,
nobly, courteously, and with a royal, just, and reasonable
heart. . . . Resolve to examine your heart often to see if
it is such toward your neighbor as you would like his to
be toward you were you in his place. This is the touch-
stone of true reason.

FRANCIS DE SALES

READY TO CARE

LUKE 10:33–34 ESV

*"But a Samaritan, as he journeyed, came to where
he was, and when he saw him, he had compassion.
He went to him and bound up his wounds, pouring
on oil and wine. Then he set him on his own animal
and brought him to an inn and took care of him."*

Again: you are called to be a meek person, not always
standing up for your rights, nor concerned to get
your own back, nor troubled in your heart by ill treatment and personal slights . . . but you are simply to commit your cause to God and leave it to him to vindicate
you if and when he sees fit. Your attitude to other people, good and bad, nice and nasty, both Christians and
unbelievers, is to be that of the good Samaritan toward
the Jew in the gutter—that is to say, your eyes must be
open to see others' needs, both spiritual and material;
your heart must be ready to care for needy souls when
you find them; your mind must be alert to plan out the
best way to help them; and your will must be set against
the trick that we are all so good at—"passing the buck,"
going by on the other side and contracting out of situations of need where sacrificial help is called for.

J. I. PACKER

THE TRUE SAMARITAN

LUKE 10:36–37 NASB

"Which of these three do you think proved to be a neighbor to the man who fell into the robbers' hands?"
And he said, "The one who showed mercy toward him." Then Jesus said to him, "Go and do the same."

By means of this parable the Lord concludes with the words, "Go, and do thou likewise," so that this lawyer did not only sin against God, but also against his neighbor. He not only failed to love God, but he did not love his neighbor, and never aid him a favor. . . .

But Christ, the true Samaritan, takes the poor man to himself as his own, goes to him and does not require the helpless one to come to him; for here is no merit, but pure grace and mercy; and he binds up his wounds, cares for him and pours in oil and wine; this is the whole gospel from beginning to end. He pours in oil when grace is preached, as when one says: Behold thou poor man, here is your unbelief, here is your condemnation. . . . All this I will cure with the gospel. Behold, here cling firmly to this Samaritan, to Christ the Savior, he will help you, and nothing else in heaven or on earth will.

MARTIN LUTHER

LOVE FOR OTHER BELIEVERS

LUKE 10:36–37 NLT
*"Now which of these three would you say was
a neighbor to the man who was attacked
by bandits?" Jesus asked. The man replied,
"The one who showed him mercy." Then Jesus said,
"Yes, now go and do the same."*

If Jesus has commanded so strongly that we love all men
as our neighbors, then how important it is especially to
love our fellow Christians. If we are told to love all men
as our neighbors—as ourselves—then surely, when it
comes to those with whom we have the special bonds as
fellow Christians—having one Father through one Jesus
Christ and being indwelt by one Spirit—we can understand how overwhelmingly important it is that all men be
able to see an observable love for those with whom we
have these special ties. Paul makes the double obligation
clear in Galatians 6:10: "As we have therefore opportunity, let us do good unto all men, especially unto them
who are of the household of faith." He does not negate
the command to do good to all men. But it is still not
meaningless to add, "especially unto them who are of the
household of faith." This dual goal should be our Christian mentality, the set of our minds.

FRANCIS A. SCHAEFFER

LOVE FOR ALL PEOPLE

LUKE 10:36–37 NIV
*"Which of these three do you think was a neighbor
to the man who fell into the hands of robbers?"
The expert in the law replied, "The one who
had mercy on him." Jesus told him,
"Go and do likewise."*

All men bear the image of God. They have value, not because they are redeemed, but because they are God's creation in God's image. Modern man, who has rejected this, has no clue as to who he is, and because of this he can find no real value for himself or for other men. . . .

All men are our neighbors, and we are to love them as ourselves. We are to do this on the basis of creation, even if they are not redeemed, for all men have value because they are made in the image of God. Therefore they are to be loved even at great cost.

This is, of course, the whole point of Jesus' story of the good Samaritan: Because a man is a man, he is to be loved at all cost.

So, when Jesus gives the special command to love our Christian brothers, it does not negate the other command. . . . The two commands reinforce each other.

FRANCIS A. SCHAEFFER

THE GOLDEN RULE

MATTHEW 7:12 NASB

*"In everything, therefore, treat people the
same way you want them to treat you,
for this is the Law and the Prophets."*

We speak of Jesus' most famous commandment as
the Golden Rule—"Do unto others as you
would have them do unto you." The fact is that this rule
existed in Judaism and in many other religions in its *negative* form—"Don't do to others what you do not want
them to do to you." In its negative form it is compara-
tively easy. It simply means that there are certain things
which we refrain from doing; but in its positive form it
means that we must go out of our way to be as kind to
others as we would have them be to us. It is not so very
difficult to refrain from doing things; but it is godlike to
do things ever in the spirit of love. The result is that the
man whose religion consists in not doing things may be
well pleased with himself; but the man whose religion
involves doing things will always feel his own failure
because he will know that he has never fully succeeded in
doing all he ought.

WILLIAM BARCLAY

THE MEANING OF LOVE

1 CORINTHIANS 13:3 NKJV

And though I bestow all my goods to feed the poor,
and though I give my body to be burned,
but have not love, it profits me nothing.

Without love good works are worthless, but with love they become wholly rewarding no matter how small and insignificant they may seem. Indeed, God places more importance on the reason you work than on how much work you actually do. A person does much who loves much; he does much who does it well; he does well who serves the common good rather than himself.

Often what seems to be love is not love at all but the natural feelings that we all have. Along with such feelings, though, usually come questionable motives, such as willfulness, the hope of reward and self-interest. The person who has pure and perfect love, however, seeks self-praise in nothing, but wishes only that God may be glorified in everything. . . . In the end, all the saints come to rest in God. Oh, a person who has even a spark of real love should truly feel all the things of this world to be of little importance, compared to God!

THOMAS À KEMPIS

TURNING YOUR MIND TOWARD GOD

DEUTERONOMY 4:7 NKJV
*"For what great nation is there that has God
so near to it, as the LORD our God is to us,
for whatever reason we may call upon Him?"*

Prayer consists in turning the mind to God. Do you wish to know how to turn your mind toward God? Follow my words. When you pray gather up your whole self, enter with your Beloved into the chamber of your heart, and there remain alone with him, forgetting all exterior concerns. And so rise aloft with all your love and all your mind, your affections, your desires, and devotion. And let not your mind wander away from your prayer, but rise again and again in the fervor of your piety until you enter into the place of the wonderful tabernacle, even the house of God. There your heart will be delighted at the sight of your Beloved and you will taste and see how good the Lord is and how great is his goodness.

ST. BONAVENTURE

GIVE WHAT YOU'VE BEEN GIVEN

PHILIPPIANS 2:4 NLT
*Don't think only about your own affairs,
but be interested in others, too,
and what they are doing.*

The truth is, that we are our best when we try to be it not for ourselves alone, but for our brethren; and that we take God's gifts most completely for ourselves when we realize that He sends them to us for the benefit of other men, who stand beyond us needing them. . . . "For their sakes I sanctify myself," said Jesus; and He hardly ever said words more wonderful than those. There was the power by which He was holy; the world was to be made holy, was to be sanctified through Him. I am sure that you or I could indeed be strengthened to meet some great experience of pain if we really believed that by our suffering we were to be made luminous with help to other men. They are to get from us painlessly what we have got most painfully from God. There is the power of the bravest martyrdom and the hardest work that the world has ever seen.

PHILLIPS BROOKS

THE WORK OF EVANGELISM

---

1 PETER 2:9 NRSV

*But you are a chosen race, a royal priesthood,
a holy nation, God's own people, in order that you
may proclaim the mighty acts of him who called
you out of darkness into his marvelous light.*

Evangelism is first of all *a work of God*. God the creator is both God the redeemer and God the evangelist. He made us; he loves us; he ransoms us; he reclaims us.

Evangelism is also a work of man or rather *a work of God through man*. God sends Christian men and women to be heralds, ambassadors, and teachers in his name and on his behalf. The task which God gives to his messengers is primarily and essentially one of proclamation but this proclamation is not to be made on a casual take-it-or-leave-it basis; the end in view is to persuade, convert, or turn the sinner.

Evangelism, again, is *a work of God through men proclaiming Jesus Christ and the new community in him*. Christian communication is not evangelism unless the full truth about Christ is preached. And the new community belongs to this central message, for the call to become a disciple is also a call to become a partner with all other disciples.

J. I. PACKER

Love Comes First

Colossians 1:7 ESV

*. . . just as you learned it from Epaphras
our beloved fellow servant. He is a faithful
minister of Christ on your behalf.*

Now as a company set apart to the name of the Lord
Jesus Christ, they were characterized by the love
which the Spirit sheds abroad in the hearts of those who
are born of God. This is all-important. To pretend to have
great zeal for the truth of the one Body, while failing to
manifest the love of the Spirit, is to put the emphasis in
the wrong place. Doctrinal correctness will never atone
for lack of brotherly love. It is far more to God who is
Himself love, in His very nature, that His people walk in
love one toward another, than that they contend valiantly
for set forms of truth, however scriptural. "Truthing in
love" (which would correctly convey the thought of
Ephesians 4:15) is more than contending for formulas. It
is the manifestation of the truth in a life of love to God
and to those who are His, as well as for poor lost sinners
for whom Christ died.

H. A. Ironside

OVERLOOK OTHERS' FAULTS

1 PETER 3:8 NKJV
Finally, all of you be of one mind,
having compassion for one another; love as brothers,
be tenderhearted, be courteous. . . .

L ove one another in spite of your differences, in spite of your faults. Love one another, and make the best of one another, as He loved us, who, for the sake of saving what was good in the human soul, forgot, forgave, put out of sight what was bad—who saw and loved what was good even in the publican Zacchaeus, even in the penitent Magdalene, even in the expiring malefactor, even in the heretical Samaritan, even in the Pharisee Nicodemus, even in the heathen soldier, even in the outcast Canaanite. It is very easy to fix our attention only on the weak points of those around us, to magnify them, to irritate them, to aggravate them; and, by so doing, we can make the burden of life unendurable, and can destroy our own and others' happiness and usefulness wherever we go. But this was not the love wherewith Christ loved us; this is not the new love wherewith we are to love one another.

ARTHUR P. STANLEY

LOVE EACH OTHER

1 THESSALONIANS 3:12 NCV
May the Lord make your love grow more and
multiply for each other and for all people so
that you will love others as we love you.

Let us see that whenever we have failed to be loving, we have also failed to be wise; that whenever we have been blind to our neighbors' interests, we have also been blind to our own; whenever we have hurt others, we have hurt ourselves still more. Let us, at this blessed Whitsuntide, ask forgiveness of God for all acts of malice and uncharitableness, blindness and hardness of heart; and pray for the spirit of true charity, which alone is true wisdom. And let us come to Holy Communion in charity with each other and with all; determined henceforth to feel for each other, and with each other; to put ourselves in our neighbors' places; to see with their eyes, and to feel with their hearts, so far as God shall give us that great grace; determined to make allowances for their mistakes and failings; to give and forgive, even as God gives and forgives, for ever; that so we may be indeed the children of our Father in heaven, whose name is Love.

CHARLES KINGSLEY

LOVE YOUR NEIGHBOR

1 PETER 3:8 NIV
Finally, all of you, live in harmony with one
another; be sympathetic, love as brothers,
be compassionate and humble.

In order for love to be genuine, it has to be above all a love for our neighbor. We must love those who are nearest to us, in our own family. From there, love spreads toward whoever may need us.

It is easy to love those who live far away. It is not always easy to love those who live right next to us. It is easier to offer a dish of rice to meet the hunger of a needy person than to comfort the loneliness and the anguish of someone in our own home who does not feel loved.

I want you to go and find the poor in your homes. Above all, your love has to start there. I want you to be the good news to those around you. I want you to be concerned about your next-door neighbor. Do you know who your neighbor is?

MOTHER TERESA

LOOK AROUND YOU

JAMES 1:27 ESV

Religion that is pure and undefiled before God, the Father, is this: to visit orphans and widows in their affliction, and to keep oneself unstained from the world.

One Christmas Eve a friend came to my house and said, "Would you like to go out with me distributing Christmas packages up in the mountains?" I was glad to go. And I was in for one of the greatest surprises of my life! I thought everybody in our community had all the necessities of life. But I was taken back into some little mountain valleys where people did not have enough to wear, enough to eat, and could not even afford soap to wash their bodies. Appalled and humbled, I asked God to forgive me for neglecting the people in my own community. I had not even bothered to look around me to see what people's needs were. . . .

There are others in our community who need a friend. There are many lonely people who never know the handclasp of a friend. They never receive a letter. They sit isolated in their loneliness. Having an interested friend willing to write to them and to visit with them would change their entire lives.

BILLY GRAHAM

DARING TO CARE

JAMES 3:17–18 NKJV
*But the wisdom that is from above is first pure,
then peaceable, gentle, willing to yield, full of
mercy and good fruits, without partiality and
without hypocrisy. Now the fruit of righteousness
is sown in peace by those who make peace.*

Every human being has a great, yet often unknown, gift to care, to be compassionate, to become present to the other, to listen, to hear, and to receive. If that gift would be set free and made available, miracles could take place. Those who really can receive bread from a stranger and smile in gratitude, can feed many without even realizing it. Those who can sit in silence with their fellow-man not knowing what to say but knowing that they should be there, can bring new life in a dying heart. . . .

To care means first of all to empty our own cup and to allow the other to come close to us. It means to take away the many barriers which prevent us from entering into communion with the other. When we dare to care, then we discover that nothing human is foreign to us, but that all the hatred and love, cruelty and compassion, fear and joy can be found in our own hearts.

HENRI NOUWEN

PICTURES OF
PRAYER

Devote yourselves to prayer,
being watchful and thankful.
COLOSSIANS 4:2 NIV

PICTURES OF PRAYER

One of Jesus' most obvious habits was prayer. Whether he was making bread, breaking bread, or healing brokenness, Jesus paused to acknowledge His Father. But Jesus went far beyond modeling prayer to teaching prayer. It comes as no surprise, then, that He told several parables to illustrate effective prayer.

Jesus' emphasis seems to have been almost solely oriented toward persistence and boldness. He offered no magic formula. The Lord's Prayer merely gives us a beautiful outline of themes, not a surefire incantation. His stories pictured prayer as a gritty, late-night determination that presses at heaven's gate. Prayer can be a widow's dogged demand for justice before a seemingly uncaring judge. Prayer takes on the tone of conflict and struggle. Work may not be prayer, but prayer is work.

The readings in this section will expose you to a fresh understanding of what it means to wrestle in prayer. As you read, examine to what degree you are willing to persevere in prayer.

HOW TO PRAY WITHOUT CEASING

LUKE 18:1 NASB
Now He was telling them a parable
to show that at all times they ought
to pray and not to lose heart.

How, then, shall we lay hold of that Life and Power and live the life of prayer without ceasing? By quiet, persistent practice in turning all of our being, day and night, in prayer and inward worship and surrender, toward him who calls in the deeps of our souls.

Mental habits of inward orientation must be established. An inner, secret turning to God can be made fairly steady after weeks and months and years of practice and lapses and failures and returns. . . .

Begin now, as you read these words, as you sit in your chair, to offer your whole selves, utterly and in joyful abandon, in quiet, glad surrender to Him who is within. . . . Walk and talk and work and laugh with your friends. But behind the scenes, keep up the life of simple prayer and inward worship. Let inward prayer be your last act before you fall asleep and the first act when you awake.

THOMAS KELLY

PASSIONATE PEOPLE

LUKE 18:2-3 NIV

He said: "In a certain town there was a judge
who neither feared God nor cared about men.
And there was a widow in that town who
kept coming to him with the plea,
'Grant me justice against my adversary.'"

Passionate people hang in there when the going gets tough. They persist, they persevere, they never lose heart, and they never quit. Proverbs 24:16 says, "For a righteous man may fall seven times and rise again." Jesus told the parable of the persistent widow "that men always ought to pray and not lose heart" (Luke 18:1). Combine these two scriptural principles, and you have the idea of a person who keeps praying and keeps persisting until success is certain—an unbeatable formula.

The apostle Paul urged that we be "not lagging in diligence, fervent in spirit, serving the Lord" (Romans 12:11). And he said to the Corinthian Christians, "But we have this treasure in earthen vessels, that the excellence of the power may be of God and not of us. . . . Therefore we do not lose heart. Even though our outward man is perishing, yet the inward man is being renewed day by day" (2 Corinthians 4:7, 16).

DAVID JEREMIAH

HE WILL ANSWER

LUKE 18:4–5 NLT

"The judge ignored her for a while, but eventually she wore him out. 'I fear neither God nor man,' he said to himself, 'but this woman is driving me crazy. I'm going to see that she gets justice, because she is wearing me out with her constant requests!'"

It looks as if he did not hear you: never mind; he does; it must be that he does; go on as the woman did; you too will be heard. She is heard at last, and in virtue of her much going; God hears at once, and will avenge speedily. The unrighteous judge cared nothing for the woman, those who cry to God are his own chosen—plain in the fact that they cry to him. He has made and appointed them to cry: they do cry: will he not hear them? They exist that they may pray; he has chosen them that they may choose him; he has called them that they may call him—that there may be such communion, such interchange as belongs to their being and the being of their Father. The gulf of indifference lay between the poor woman and the unjust judge; God and those who seek his help, are closer than two hands clasped hard in love: he will avenge them speedily.

GEORGE MACDONALD

WAITING

LUKE 18:7 NIV
"And will not God bring about justice for his chosen ones, who cry out to him day and night? Will he keep putting them off?"

Waiting is part of ordinary time. We discover God in our waiting: waiting in checkout lines, waiting for the telephone to ring, waiting for graduation, waiting for a promotion, waiting to retire, waiting to die. The waiting itself becomes prayer as we give our waiting to God. In waiting we begin to get in touch with the rhythms of life—stillness and action, listening and decision. They are the rhythms of God. It is in the everyday and the commonplace that we learn patience, acceptance, and contentment. . . .

In a world in which *Winning Through Intimidation* is the order of the day, I am attracted to people who are free from the tyranny of assertiveness. I am drawn to those who are able to simply meet people where they are, with no need to control or manage or make them do anything. I enjoy being around them because they draw the best out in me without any manipulation whatsoever.

RICHARD J. FOSTER

THE GOODNESS OF GOD

LUKE 18:7–8 NKJV

"And shall God not avenge His own elect
who cry out day and night to Him,
though He bears long with them? I tell you
that He will avenge them speedily."

We pray to God to know his passion, death, and resurrection—which come from the goodness of God. We pray to God for the strength that comes from his Cross—which also comes from the goodness of God. We pray to God with all the help of the saints who have gone before us—which, again, comes from the goodness of God. All of the strength that may come through prayer comes from the goodness of God, for he is the goodness of everything. For the highest form of prayer is to the goodness of God. It comes down to us to meet our humblest needs. It gives life to our souls and makes them live and grow in grace and virtue. It is near in nature and swift in grace, for it is the same grace which our souls seek and always will.

JULIAN OF NORWICH

THE FATHER'S LOVE

LUKE 18:7–8 NRSV

*"And will not God grant justice to his chosen ones
who cry to him day and night? Will he delay
long in helping them? I tell you, he will quickly
grant justice to them. And yet, when the
Son of Man comes, will he find faith on earth?"*

When you go to prayer, your first thought must be:
The Father is in secret, the Father waits me there.
Just because your heart is cold and prayerless, get you into
the presence of the loving Father. As a father pitieth his
children, so the Lord pitieth you. Do not be thinking of
how little you have to bring God, but of how much He
wants to give you. Just place yourself before Him, and
look up into His face; think of His love, His wonderful,
tender, pitying love. Tell Him how sinful and cold and
dark all is; it is the Father's loving heart will give light and
warmth to yours.

ANDREW MURRAY

PRAYING AWAY SIN

LUKE 18:1–7 NIV

*Then Jesus told his disciples a parable to show them
that they should always pray and not give up. He said:
"In a certain town there was a judge who neither feared
God nor cared about men. And there was a widow in
that town who kept coming to him with the plea, 'Grant
me justice against my adversary.' For some time he
refused. But finally he said to himself, 'Even though I
don't fear God or care about men, yet because this
widow keeps bothering me, I will see that she gets
justice, so that she won't eventually wear me out with
her coming!'" And the Lord said, "Listen to what the
unjust judge says. And will not God bring about justice
for his chosen ones, who cry out to him day and night?"*

Finally, and perhaps best of all, I believed anew what is
taught us in the parable of the Unjust Judge. No evil
habit is so ingrained nor so long prayed against (as it
seemed) in vain, that it cannot, even in dry old age, be
whisked away.

C. S. LEWIS

RESTING IN PRAYER

PSALM 61:4 NASB
Let me dwell in Your tent forever;
Let me take refuge in the shelter of Your wings.

I cannot help the thought which grows steadily upon
me, that the better part of prayer is not the asking, but
the kneeling where we can ask, the resting there, the stay-
ing there, drawing out the willing moments in heavenly
communion with God, within the closet, with the night
changed into the brightness of the day by the light of
Him who all the night was in prayer to God. Just to be
there, at leisure from ourselves, at leisure from the world,
with our souls at liberty, with our spirit feeling its kinship
to the Divine Spirit, with our life finding itself in the life
of God—this is prayer. Would it be possible that one
could be thus with God, listening to Him, speaking to
Him, reposing upon His love, and not come out with a
shining face, a gladdened heart, an intent more constant
and more strong to give to the waiting world which so
sadly needs it what has been taken from the heart of God?

ALEXANDER MCKENZIE

THE BURDEN OF SELF

PSALM 25:17 NRSV
*Relieve the troubles of my heart,
and bring me out of my distress.*

The greatest burden we have to carry in life is self. The most difficult thing we have to manage is self. Our own daily living, our frames and feelings, our especial weaknesses and temptations, and our peculiar temperaments, our inward affairs of every kind—these are the things that perplex and worry us more than anything else, and that bring us oftenest into bondage and darkness. In laying off your burdens, therefore, the first one you must get rid of is yourself. You must hand yourself and all your inward experiences, your temptations, your temperament, your frames and feelings, all over into the care and keeping of your God, and leave them there. He made you and therefore He understands you, and knows how to manage you, and you must trust Him to do it.

HANNAH WHITALL SMITH

WAITING ON GOD

EPHESIANS 3:19 NIV
*. . . and to know this love that surpasses
knowledge—that you may be filled to
the measure of all the fullness of God.*

In praying, we are often occupied with ourselves, with
our own needs, and our own efforts in the presentation
of them. In waiting upon God, the first thought is of *the
God upon whom we wait.* God longs to reveal Himself, to
fill us with Himself. Waiting on God gives Him time in
His own way and divine power to come to us. Before you
pray, bow quietly before God, to remember and realize
who He is, how near He is, how certainly He can and
will help. Be still before Him, and allow His Holy Spirit
to waken and stir up in your soul the childlike disposition
of absolute dependence and confident expectation. Wait
on God till you know you have met Him; prayer will then
become so different. And when you are praying, let there
be intervals of silence, reverent stillness of soul, in which
you yield yourself to God, in case He may have aught He
wishes to teach you or to work in you.

ANDREW MURRAY

ALWAYS BE PRAYERFUL

ROMANS 12:12 NLT
Be glad for all God is planning for you.
Be patient in trouble, and always be prayerful.

Prayer is a preparation for danger, it is the armor for battle. Go not into the dangerous world without it. You kneel down at night to pray and drowsiness weighs down your eyelids. A hard day's work is a kind of excuse, and you shorten your prayer, and resign yourself softly to repose. The morning breaks, and it may be you rise late, and so your early devotions are not done, or done with irregular haste. It is no marvel if that day in which you suffer drowsiness to interfere with prayer be a day on which you betray Him by cowardice and soft shrinking from duty.

FREDERICK W. ROBERTSON

ASKING IN JESUS' NAME

1 JOHN 5:14 NKJV
*Now this is the confidence that we have in Him,
that if we ask anything according to His will,
He hears us.*

The aim of prayer is not to force God's hand or make him do our will against his own, but to deepen our knowledge of him and our fellowship with him through contemplating his glory, confessing our dependence and need, and consciously embracing his goals. Our asking therefore must be *according to God's will* and *in Jesus' name*. . . .

To ask in Jesus' name is not to use a verbal spell but to base our asking on Christ's saving relationship to us through the cross; this will involve making petitions which Christ can endorse and put his name to. . . .

Central to the life of prayer is letting ourselves be taught by Christ through his Word and Spirit what we should pray for. To the extent that we know, through the Spirit's inner witness, that we are making a request which the Lord has specifically given us to make, to that extent we *know* that we have the answer even before we see it.

J. I. PACKER

FORGETTING TO PRAY

EPHESIANS 6:18 NCV

*Pray in the Spirit at all times with all kinds of prayers,
asking for everything you need. To do this
you must always be ready and never give up.
Always pray for all God's people.*

Lord, I confess this morning I remembered my breakfast, but forgot my prayers. And as I have returned no
praise, so thou mightst justly have afforded me no protec-
tion. Yet thou hast carefully kept me to the middle of this
day, [entrusting] me with a new debt before I have paid
the old score. It is now noon, too late for a morning, too
soon for an evening sacrifice. My corrupt heart prompts
me to put off my prayers till night; but I know it too well,
or rather too ill, to trust it. I fear if I defer them till night,
at night I shall forget them. Be pleased, therefore, now to
accept them. Lord, let not a few hours the later make a
breach, especially seeing (be it spoken not to excuse my
negligence, but to implore thy pardon) a thousand years
in thy sight are but as yesterday. I promise hereafter, by thy
assistance, to bring forth fruit in due season.

THOMAS FULLER

PRAYER AND THE MODERN WORLD

LUKE 11:5–6 NIV

*Then he said to them, "Suppose one of you has a
friend, and he goes to him at midnight and says,
'Friend, lend me three loaves of bread, because a
friend of mine on a journey has come to me,
and I have nothing to set before him.'"*

Although this parable is concerned with the power of
persistent prayer, it may also serve as a basis for our
thought concerning many contemporary problems and
the role of the church in grappling with them. It is midnight in the parable; it is also midnight in our world, and
the darkness is so deep that we can hardly see which way
to turn. . . .

If the church does not participate actively in the struggle for peace and for economic and racial justice, it will
forfeit the loyalty of millions and cause men everywhere
to say that it has atrophied its will. But if the church will
free itself from the shackles of a deadening status quo, and,
recovering its great historic mission, will speak and act
fearlessly and insistently in terms of justice and peace, it
will enkindle the imagination of mankind and fire the
souls of men, imbuing them with a glowing and ardent
love for truth, justice, and peace.

MARTIN LUTHER KING, JR.

THE STRUGGLE OF PRAYER

LUKE 11:7 NRSV

*"And he answers from within, 'Do not bother me;
the door has already been locked, and my children
are with me in bed; I cannot get up
and give you anything.'"*

Prayer, though from one standpoint the most natural thing a Christian ever does, since crying to his heavenly Father is a Spirit-wrought instinct in him, is always a battle against distractions, discouragements, and deadenings from Satan and from our own sinfulness. God may actually resist us when we pray in order that we in turn may resist and overcome his resistance, and so be led into deeper dependence on him and greater enrichment from him at the end of the day (think of wrestling Jacob, and clamoring Job, and the parable of the unjust judge). I see true prayer, like all true obedience, as a constant struggle in which you make headway by effort against what opposes, and however much you progress you are always aware of imperfection, incompleteness, and how much further you have to go.

J. I. PACKER

PERSEVERE

LUKE 11:8 NASB

*"I tell you, even though he will not get up and
give him anything because he is his friend,
yet because of his persistence he will get up
and give him as much as he needs."*

First, "Continue steadfastly in prayer." There is so much power to be had in persevering prayer. Don't forget the "importunate friend" of Luke 11:8 ("Because of his persistence he will get up and give him as much as he needs" NASB), and don't forget the parable Jesus told to the effect that we "ought always to pray and not lose heart" (Luke 18:1–8). Perseverance is the great test of genuineness in the Christian life. I praise God for Christians who have persevered in prayer sixty, seventy, or eighty years! Oh, let us be a praying people, and let this year—and all our years—be saturated with prayers to the Lord of all power and all good. It will be good to say in the end, "I have finished the race, I have kept the faith"— through prayer.

JOHN PIPER

PRAY SHAMELESSLY

LUKE 11:8 NKJV
"I say to you, though he will not rise and give to him because he is his friend, yet because of his persistence he will rise and give him as many as he needs."

The man must feed his friend, for hospitality is a sacred duty. So he goes to another friend for *three loaves*, i.e., three small loaves which would suffice for one man. But this second householder has shut his door and gone to bed with his children. . . . He raises no difficulty about giving the bread, but the bother of getting up is quite another matter. . . .

But the man is persistent. He will not go away, nor will he let his friend go back to sleep. And where friendship cannot prevail, *his importunity* (lit. 'shamelessness') wins the day. The lesson is clear. We must not play at prayer, but must show persistence if we do not receive the answer immediately. It is not that God is unwilling and must be pressed into answering. . . . But if we do not want what we are asking for enough to be persistent, we do not want it very much. It is not such tepid prayer that is answered.

LEON MORRIS

A MIGHTY WEAPON

LUKE 11:8 KJV

I say unto you, Though he will not rise and give him, because he is his friend, yet because of his importunity he will rise and give him as many as he needeth.

Prayer is a mighty weapon if it is done in the right mindset. Prayer is so strong that continual pleas have overcome shamelessness, injustice, and savage cruelty. . . . It has also overcome laziness and things that friendship could not bring about. For, "although he will not give him because he is his friend, yet because of his appeals he will rise and give to him." In addition, continual requests made an unworthy woman worthy. . . .

Let us pray diligently. Prayer is a mighty weapon if used with earnestness and sincerity, without drawing attention to ourselves. It has turned back wars and benefited an entire undeserving nation. . . . So then, if we pray with humility, beating our chests like the tax gatherer and saying what he did, "Be merciful to me a sinner," we will obtain everything we ask for. . . . We need much repentance, beloved, much prayer, much endurance, and much perseverance to gain the good things that have been promised to us.

JOHN CHRYSOSTOM

COMMUNION WITH GOD

LUKE 11:9 NCV
*"So I tell you, ask, and God will give
to you. Search, and you will find. Knock,
and the door will open for you."*

Prayer, is first of all, communion with God. Our blessed Lord Himself, in the days of His flesh, is seen again and again leaving the company of His disciples and going out into some desert place on a mountainside, or into a garden, that His spirit might be refreshed as He bowed in prayer alone with the Father. From such seasons of fellowship He returned to do His mightiest works and to bear witness to the truth. And in this He is our great Exemplar. . . .

We are told to continue in prayer. This does not mean that we are to be constantly teasing God in order that we may obtain what we might think would add most to our happiness or be best for us, but we are to abide in a sense of His presence and of our dependence upon His bounty. We are to learn to talk to Him and to quietly wait before Him, too, in order that we may hear His voice as He speaks to us.

H. A. IRONSIDE

CHILDLIKE PRAYER

LUKE 11:9 NIV
*"So I say to you: Ask and it will be given
to you; seek and you will find; knock
and the door will be opened to you."*

Nothing is more central to the spiritual life than prayer, for prayer ushers us into perpetual communion with the heart of God. And there are many things to learn about this life of constant conversation with the Holy One.

But we must beware of making things too complicated. Like children coming to their parents, so we come to God. There is awe to be sure, but there is also intimacy. We bring our heart cries to a loving Father. Like the mother hen who gathers her chicks under her wings, so our God cares for us, protects us, comforts us (Matt. 23:37).

So no matter how much we study the labyrinthine realities of prayer, let us forever come as children to a loving Abba who delights to give and to forgive.

RICHARD J. FOSTER

PRAYERLESSNESS

ISAIAH 64:7 NLT
Yet no one calls on your name or pleads with you
for mercy. Therefore, you have turned away
from us and turned us over to our sins.

The worst sin is prayerlessness. Overt sin, or crime, or
the glaring inconsistencies which often surprise us in
Christian people are the effect of this, or its punishment.
We are left by God for lack of seeking Him. The history
of the saints shows often that their lapses were the fruit
and nemesis of slackness or neglect in prayer. . . . Trusting
the God of Christ, and transacting with Him, we come
into tune with men. . . . Prayer is an act, indeed *the* act, of
fellowship. We cannot truly pray even for ourselves without passing beyond ourselves and our individual experience. . . . Not to want to pray, then, is the sin behind sin.
And it ends in not being able to pray. . . . We do not take
our spiritual food, and so we falter, dwindle, and die. 'In
the sweat of your brow ye shall eat your bread.' That has
been said to be true both of physical and spiritual labor.

PETER TAYLOR FORSYTH

PAY ATTENTION

LUKE 11:9 NLT
*"And so I tell you, keep on asking, and
you will be given what you ask for. Keep on looking,
and you will find. Keep on knocking,
and the door will be opened."*

"Blessed are the drowsy ones for they shall soon drop off to sleep!" wrote Nietzsche, and his satirical warning holds for those who do not pray. For prayer is awakeness, attention, intense inward openness. In a certain way sin could be described, and described with a good deal of penetration, by noting that it is anything that destroys this attention. Pride, self-will, self-absorption, doublemindedness, dishonesty, sexual excess, overeating, overdrinking, overactivity of any sort, all destroy attention and all cut the nerve of effective prayer. Just as sleep is upset by any serious mental disturbance, so attention is dispersed when unfaced sin gets the ascendancy. If prayer is attention, then it is naturally attention to the highest thing that I know, to my "ultimate concern," and this human prayer means a moving out of a life of inattention, out of the dispersion, out of "the Gethsemane sleep" into the life of openness and attention to the highest that I know. God can only disclose the Divine whispers to those who are attending.

DOUGLAS V. STEERE

GIVE GOD YOUR WHOLE LIFE

LUKE 11:10 NIV

"For everyone who asks receives; he who seeks finds;
and to him who knocks, the door will be opened."

Now if we conclude that we must be pious in our prayers, we must also conclude that we must be pious in all the other aspects of our lives. For there is no reason why we should make God the rule and measure of our prayers, why we should look wholly unto him and pray according to his will, and yet not make him the rule and measure of all the other actions of our life. For any ways of life, any employment of our talents whether of our bodies, our time, or money that are not strictly according to the will of God, that are not done to his glory are simply absurdities, and our prayers fail because they are not according to the will of God. . . . It is our strict duty to live by reason, to devote all of the action of our lives to God. . . . If our prayers do not lead us to this, they are of no value no matter how wise or heavenly.

WILLIAM LAW

PRAYING THE PSALMS

PSALM 13:1 ESV
How long, O LORD? Will you forget me forever?
How long will you hide your face from me?

The Bible contains many recorded models of prayer—
150 psalms, the Lord's Prayer, and the prayers of
saints from Abraham to Paul. . . .

As for the Psalms, I am always intrigued to find how
Christians relate to them, for it took me years after my
conversion to feel at home in them. Why? Partly, I think,
because the view of life as a battle which the Psalms
embody took longer to root itself in my heart than in my
head; partly because the middle-class misconception that
tidiness, self-conscious balance, and restraint are essentials
of godliness—a misconception which makes most of the
Psalms seem uncouth—possessed both my head and my
heart for longer. More and more, however, the psalmists'
calls for help, their complaints, confessions of sin, depres-
sion, celebrations of God, cries of love for him, challenges
and commitments to him, and hopes placed exclusively in
him, have become the emotional world of my prayers and
I think this is how it should be.

J. I. PACKER

PRAY WITHOUT CEASING

1 THESSALONIANS 5:17 NIV
Pray continually.

Our thinking about prayer, whether right or wrong, is based on our own mental conception of it. The correct concept is to think of prayer as the breath in our lungs and the blood from our hearts. Our blood flows and our breathing continues "without ceasing;" we are not even conscious of it, but it never stops. And we are not always conscious of Jesus keeping us in perfect oneness with God, but if we are obeying Him, He always is. Prayer is not an exercise, it is the life of the saint. Beware of anything that stops the offering up of prayer. "Pray without ceasing . . ."—maintain the childlike habit of offering up prayer in your heart to God all the time.

OSWALD CHAMBERS

A LIFE OF PRAYER

1 THESSALONIANS 5:17–18 NRSV
*Pray without ceasing, give thanks in all
circumstances; for this is the will of God
in Christ Jesus for you.*

Let us not be content to pray morning and evening,
but let us live in prayer all day long. Let this prayer,
this life of love, which means death to self, spread out
from our seasons of prayer, as from a centre, over all that
we have to do. All should become prayer, that is, a loving
consciousness of God's presence, whether it be social
intercourse or business. Such a course as this will ensure
you a profound peace.

FRANÇOIS FÉNELON

PERSISTENCE IN PRAYER

MATTHEW 7:7–8 NIV

*"Ask and it will be given to you; seek and you will
find; knock and the door will be opened to you.
For everyone who asks receives; he who seeks finds;
and to him who knocks, the door will be opened."*

This is the lesson of the parable in Luke 18:1–8 about
the widow. She was so persistent and importunate in
her refusal to let go of the judge that he was overpowered
and had to help her in spite of himself. How much more,
Christ argues there (Luke 18:7), will God give us if He
sees that we do not stop praying but go right on knocking so that He has to hear it? This is all the more so
because He has promised to do so and shows that such
persistence is pleasing to Him. Since your need goes right
on knocking, therefore, you go right on knocking, too,
and do not relent. . . . By urging you not only to ask but
also to knock, God intends to test you to see whether you
can hold on tight, and to teach you that your prayer is not
displeasing to Him or unheard, simply because His answer
is delayed and you are permitted to go on seeking and
knocking.

MARTIN LUTHER

PRAY LIKE THIS

MATTHEW 6:9 ESV
*"Pray then like this:
'Our Father in heaven,
hallowed be your name.'"*

N o man will pray aright, unless his lips and heart shall be directed by the Heavenly Master. For that purpose he has laid down this rule, by which we must frame our prayers. . . .

This form of prayer consists, as I have said, of six petitions. The first three, it ought to be known, relate to the glory of God, without any regard to ourselves; and the remaining three relate to those things which are necessary for our salvation. As the law of God is divided into two tables, of which the former contains the duties of piety, and the latter the duties of charity, so in prayer Christ enjoins us to consider and seek the glory of God, and, at the same time, permits us to consult our own interests. Let us therefore know, that we shall be in a state of mind for praying in a right manner, if we not only are in earnest about ourselves and our own advantage, but assign the first place to the glory of God.

JOHN CALVIN

THE NECESSITY OF PRAYER

JAMES 5:13–15 NASB
Is anyone among you suffering? Then he must pray.
Is anyone cheerful? He is to sing praises. Is anyone
among you sick? Then he must call for the elders of
the church and they are to pray over him, anointing
him with oil in the name of the Lord; and the prayer
offered in faith will restore the one who is sick,
and the Lord will raise him up, and if he has
committed sins, they will be forgiven him.

Words fail to explain how necessary prayer is . . .
Surely, with good reason the Heavenly Father
affirms that the only stronghold of safety is in calling upon
his name [cf. Joel 2:32]. By so doing we invoke the presence both of his providence, through which he watches
over and guards our affairs, and of his power, through
which he sustains us, weak as we are and well-nigh overcome, and of his goodness, through which he receives us,
miserably burdened with sins, unto grace; and, in short, it
is by prayer that we call him to reveal himself as wholly
present to us. Hence comes an extraordinary peace and
repose to our consciences. For having disclosed to the
Lord the necessity that was pressing upon us, we even rest
fully in the thought that none of our ills is hid from him
who, we are convinced, has both the will and the power
to take the best care of us.

JOHN CALVIN

IN SPIRIT AND IN TRUTH

JOHN 4:24 NKJV
*"God is Spirit, and those who worship Him
must worship in spirit and truth."*

You do not feel in the spirit of prayer; you have no
spiritual uplift; you are simply indifferent. Give that
unhappy mood no heed. You know very well what you
ought to do. You ought to present yourself before God;
you ought to say your prayers. Do that, and the devout
attitude, the bended knees, the folded hands, the quiet
and the silence, the lips busied with holy words, will
induce the consciousness of the divine presence, and help
you to pray in spirit and in truth.

GEORGE HODGES

THE SERVICE OF PRAYER

1 SAMUEL 12:23 ESV

*"Moreover, as for me, far be it from me that I should
sin against the LORD by ceasing to pray for you,
and I will instruct you in the good and the right way."*

Perhaps we do not think enough [about] what an effective service prayer is, especially intercessory prayer. We do not believe as we should how it might help those we so fain would serve, penetrating the hearts we cannot open, shielding those we cannot guard, teaching where we cannot speak, comforting where our words have no power to soothe; following the steps of our beloved through the toils and perplexities of the day, lifting off their burdens with an unseen hand at night. No ministry is so like that of an angel as this—silent, invisible, known but to God.

ELIZABETH RUNDLE CHARLES

GIVE GOD YOUR TROUBLES

PSALM 32:6–7 NRSV

Therefore let all who are faithful offer prayer
to you; at a time of distress, the rush of mighty
waters shall not reach them. You are a hiding
place for me; you preserve me from trouble;
you surround me with glad cries of deliverance.

What are the things we should lay before the Almighty God in prayer? Answer: First, our personal troubles. In Psalm 32, David cried out, "You are my hiding place; you will protect me from trouble and surround me with songs of deliverance" (v. 7). Likewise, in Psalm 142, "I cry aloud to the Lord . . . I pour out my complaint before him; before him I tell my trouble." When we pray we should keep in mind all of the shortcomings and excesses we feel, and pour them out freely to God, our faithful Father, who is ready to help. If you do not know or recognize your needs, or think you have none, then you are in the worst possible place. The greatest trouble we can ever know is thinking that we have no trouble for we have become hard-hearted and insensible to what is inside of us.

MARTIN LUTHER

THE GOD OF OUR LORD JESUS CHRIST

EPHESIANS 1:15–17 ESV

*For this reason, because I have heard of your faith
in the Lord Jesus and your love toward all the saints,
I do not cease to give thanks for you, remembering you
in my prayers, that the God of our Lord Jesus Christ,
the Father of glory, may give you a spirit of wisdom
and of revelation in the knowledge of him.*

So when Paul reminds himself that he is praying to 'the God of our Lord Jesus Christ' he reminds himself that he is praying to the God of our salvation, he is praying to the God who has originated and brought to pass all the things we have been considering from verse 3 to verse 14 in our chapter. He is praying to the God who has, before the foundation of the world, chosen and elected us and planned His glorious purpose in Christ for our final complete salvation. What a difference it makes to prayer when you begin in that manner! You no longer go to God uncertainly, or with doubts and queries as to whether He is going to receive you; you remember and realize that you are praying because He has done something to you, and drawn you to Himself in and through 'our Lord Jesus Christ.'

DAVID MARTYN LLOYD-JONES

THE SPIRIT INTERCEDES FOR US

ROMANS 8:26 NIV

In the same way, the Spirit helps us in our weakness.
We do not know what we ought to pray for,
but the Spirit himself intercedes for us
with groans that words cannot express.

If our prayer reach or move Him it is because He first reached and moved us to pray. The prayer that reached heaven began there, when Christ went forth. It began when God turned to beseech us in Christ—in the appealing Lamb slain before the foundation of the world. The Spirit went out with the power and function in it to return with our soul. Our prayer is the answer to God's. . . . The whole rhythm of Christ's soul, so to say, was Godhead going out and returning on itself. And so God stirs and inspires all prayer which finds and moves Him. His love provokes our sacred forwardness. . . . All say, 'I am yours if you will;' and when we will it is prayer. Any final glory of human success or destiny rises from man being God's continual creation, and destined by Him for Him. So we pray because we were made for prayer, and God draws us out by breathing Himself in.

P. T. FORSYTH

SOLITUDE

MATTHEW 6:6 NLT

*"But when you pray, go away by yourself, shut the
door behind you, and pray to your Father secretly.
Then your Father, who knows all secrets,
will reward you."*

Without solitude it is virtually impossible to live a
spiritual life. Solitude begins with a time and place
for God, and him alone. If we really believe not only that
God exists but also that he is actively present in our
lives—healing, teaching, and guiding—we need to set
aside a time and space to give him our undivided attention. . . .

Once we have committed ourselves to spending time
in solitude, we develop an attentiveness to God's voice in
us. In the beginning, during the first days, weeks, or even
months, we may have the feeling that we are simply wasting our time. Time in solitude may at first seem little
more than a time in which we are bombarded by thou-
sands of thoughts and feelings that emerge from hidden
areas of our mind. . . . At first, the many distractions keep
presenting themselves. Later, as they receive less and less
attention, they slowly withdraw.

HENRI NOUWEN

PRAYER FOR OTHERS

EPHESIANS 6:18 NASB

*With all prayer and petition pray at all times
in the Spirit, and with this in view, be on the alert
with all perseverance and petition for all the saints.*

Prayer for others is a form of petitional prayer that makes deep demands on the faith of an individualistic generation that has so largely lost its sense of inner community. Yet at no point do we touch the inner springs of prayer more vitally than here. For when we hold up the life of another before God, when we expose it to God's love, when we pray for its release from drowsiness, for the quickening of its inner health, for the power to throw off a destructive habit, for the restoration of its free and vital relationship with its fellows, for its strength to resist a temptation, for its courage to continue against sharp opposition—only then do we sense what it means to share in God's work, in His concern; only then do the walls that separate us from others go down and we sense that we are at bottom all knit together in a great and intimate family.

DOUGLAS V. STEERE

THE LORD'S PRAYER

MATTHEW 6:10–12 NRSV

Your kingdom come. Your will be done, on earth as it is in heaven. Give us this day our daily bread. And forgive us our debts, as we also have forgiven our debtors.

Your will be done, on earth as it is in heaven.

May we love you with our whole heart by always thinking of you, with our whole soul by always desiring you, with our whole mind by directing all our intentions to you, and with our whole strength by spending all our energies in your service. And may we love our neighbors as ourselves. . . .

Give us this day our daily bread.

In memory and understanding and reverence of the love which our Lord Jesus Christ has for us, revealed by his sacrifice for us on the cross, we ask for the perfect bread of his body.

And forgive us our trespasses.

We know that you forgive us, through the suffering and death of your beloved Son.

As we forgive those who trespass against us.

Enable us to forgive perfectly and without reserve any wrong that has been committed against us.

ST. FRANCIS OF ASSISI

Prayer from the Heart

Philippians 4:6–7 tlb

Don't worry about anything; instead, pray about everything; tell God your needs and don't forget to thank him for his answers. If you do this you will experience God's peace, which is far more wonderful than the human mind can understand. His peace will keep your thoughts and your hearts quiet and at rest as you trust in Christ Jesus.

God is a Spirit, *said Jesus Christ,* and they that worship him must worship him in spirit and in truth. *Prayer then is in itself a wholly spiritual act, addressed to him who is the Supreme Spirit, the Spirit who sees all things and is present in all things and is, as St. Augustine says, more closely united to our soul than its deepest depths. If to this essential prayer we join a particular attitude of the body and certain words and outward demonstrations, all this has no significance in itself and is only pleasing to God as it expresses the feelings of the heart. To speak properly, it is the heart that prays, it is to the voice of the heart that God listens and it is the heart that he answers, and when we speak of the heart we mean the most spiritual part of us. It is indeed noteworthy that in the Scriptures prayer is always ascribed to the heart.*

Jean-Nicolas Grou

PRAYING THE LORD'S PRAYER TODAY

LUKE 11:2 NIV

He said to them, "When you pray, say:
'Father, hallowed be your name,
your kingdom come.'"

What then might it mean to pray this kingdom prayer today? It means, for a start, that as we look up into the face of our Father in heaven, and commit ourselves to the hallowing of his name, we look immediately out upon the whole world that he made, and we see it as he sees it. . . . It means seeing it with the love of the Creator for his spectacularly beautiful creation, and seeing it with the deep grief of the Creator for the battered and battle-scarred state in which the world now finds itself. . . .

We are praying, as Jesus was praying and acting, for the redemption of the world. . . . And if we pray this way, we must of course be prepared to live this way.

So, as we pray this for the world, we also pray for the church. . . . Make us a community of healed healers; make us a retuned orchestra to play the kingdom-music until the world takes up the song.

N. T. WRIGHT

MORNING PRAYER

PSALM 5:3 NLT
Listen to my voice in the morning, LORD.
Each morning I bring my requests
to you and wait expectantly.

The entire day receives order and discipline when it acquires unity. This unity must be sought and found in morning prayer. It is confirmed in work. The morning prayer determines the day. Squandered time of which we are ashamed, temptations to which we succumb, weaknesses and lack of courage in work, disorganization and lack of discipline in our thoughts and in our conversation with other men, all have their origin most often in the neglect of morning prayer.

Order and distribution of our time become more firm where they originate in prayer. Temptations which accompany the working day will be conquered on the basis of the morning breakthrough to God. Decisions, demanded by work, become easier and simpler where they are made not in the fear of men but only in the sight of God. . . . Even mechanical work is done in a more patient way if it arises from the recognition of God and his command. The powers to work take hold, therefore, at the place where we have prayed to God.

DIETRICH BONHOEFFER

PICTURES OF HUMILITY

God opposes the proud
but gives grace to the humble.

JAMES 4:6 NIV

PICTURES OF HUMILITY

Humility is a tricky character trait. Beware of the temptation to declare that you are not humble. That statement assumes you would recognize it in yourself if you possessed it. Better to admit pride, a wiser course to take when you long to grow in humility. Pride will always be a more persistent companion. Knowing and acknowledging your pride will keep humility from being a problem.

Jesus taught us not to claim but to practice humility. The illustrations He used are filled with risk. If we choose to take an unimportant place or role, others may not praise us but ignore us. If we choose to serve, we may be treated as servants. Our response at that point will give us some indication of the difficulty of humility. Note in the readings that follow how quickly humility vanishes under the glare of comparison with others. Those who seek to know Jesus well and to obey Him will often grow in humility because they aren't thinking about it much.

HUMILITY AND FAITH

2 CHRONICLES 7:14 NRSV

"If my people who are called by my name humble
themselves, pray, seek my face, and turn from
their wicked ways, then I will hear from heaven,
and will forgive their sin and heal their land."

It's the humility that brings a soul to be nothing before
God that also removes every hindrance to faith. . . .

Christian, have we not here the cause of failure in the
pursuit of holiness? . . . We had no idea to what an extent
pride and self were still secretly working within us, and
how Christ alone by His incoming and His mighty power
could cast them out. We did not understand that nothing
but the new and divine nature, taking entirely the place
of the old self, could make us really humble. We did not
know that absolute, unceasing, universal humility must be
the basic attitude of every prayer and every approach to
God, as well as of every dealing with people. Nor did we
know that we might as well attempt to see without eyes
or live without breath, as to believe or draw near to God
or dwell in His love without an all-pervading humility
and lowliness of heart.

ANDREW MURRAY

THE PATH TO HUMILITY

ACTS 9:3–5 NIV
*As he neared Damascus on his journey, suddenly
a light from heaven flashed around him.
He fell to the ground. . . . "Who are you, Lord?"
Saul asked. "I am Jesus, whom you
are persecuting," he replied.*

Virtually all Christians pass through two stages in their pursuit of humility. In the first they fear and flee and seek deliverance from all that can humble them. They haven't yet learned to seek humility at any cost. They have accepted the command to be humble, and seek to obey it, but they only discover how completely they fail. At times they pray very earnestly for humility. But in their heart they pray more—if not in word then in wish—to be kept from the very things that will make them humble.

They are not yet so in love with humility—esteeming it as the beauty of the Lamb of God and the joy of heaven—that they would sell all to procure it. . . .

But can we hope to reach the second stage in which this will be the case? Undoubtedly. And what will it be that brings us there? That which brought Paul there—a new revelation of the Lord Jesus Christ.

ANDREW MURRAY

WHAT CHRIST DEMANDS

LUKE 14:7–8 NKJV

*So He told a parable to those who were invited,
when He noted how they chose the best places,
saying to them: "When you are invited by
anyone to a wedding feast, do not sit down
in the best place. . . ."*

Jesus' words are still revolutionary today because they challenge our human tendency to build our lives in an egocentric, self-satisfied way. The things I do, the decisions I make, are usually chosen to meet my own needs and to promote my own self-image. And when I examine myself, I'm usually pretty pleased with what I see. . . .

But Christ challenges this complacent self-image. He demands more of us. We can't just fulfill the letter of God's commandments (difficult though that is to do at times); we must also fulfill its spirit, in our words and thoughts as well as our deeds.

It's not only a revolutionary message but an expansive one. If we want to follow Christ, the Sermon on the Mount tells us how: it requires us to enlarge our understanding of words such as *forgiveness, honesty, justice, compassion,* and *love.* Is it easy to do? No! But it's the avenue—the only avenue—to personal peace and peace in our world.

JIMMY CARTER

DON'T EXALT YOURSELF

LUKE 14:8-9 NASB

*"When you are invited by someone to a wedding feast,
do not take the place of honor, for someone more
distinguished than you may have been invited by him,
and he who invited you both will come and
say to you, 'Give your place to this man,' and then
in disgrace you proceed to occupy the last place."*

Usually the exact hour of a feast was not specified. Those who were eager and grateful for the invitation usually came early, while those who had a good conceit of their own importance usually came late so that all could see their arrival. It was therefore very common for the people who were socially unimportant to be there early and for the really important guests to arrive last. If then one of the early comers were to take one of the highest and most honourable places the chances were that he would be asked to move when the honoured guests arrived. So Jesus' advice was that when a man was invited to a feast he should not set himself down in a place of honour lest he had the shame of being asked to move down to make way for someone more important. Rather he should take the lowest place he could find so that he might be invited to move up and so be honoured in the presence of his fellow guests.

WILLIAM BARCLAY

TAKE THE LOWEST PLACE

LUKE 14:10 NRSV

*"But when you are invited, go and sit down at
the lowest place, so that when your host comes,
he may say to you, 'Friend, move up higher';
then you will be honoured in the presence
of all who sit at the table with you."*

Jesus commands Christians to seek consciously the
lowest room. All of us—pastors, teachers, professional
religious workers and nonprofessional included—are
tempted to say, "I will take the larger place because it will
give me more influence for Jesus Christ." Both individual
Christians and Christian organizations fall prey to the
temptation of rationalizing this way as we build bigger
and bigger empires. But according to the Scripture this is
backwards: we should consciously take the lowest place
unless the Lord Himself extrudes us into a greater one.

FRANCIS A. SCHAEFFER

RESPONDING TO JESUS

LUKE 14:11 NIV

"For everyone who exalts himself will be humbled,
and he who humbles himself will be exalted."

Can you imagine that scene? I'm sure that after the Lord spoke, no servant moved, no dish clattered. Silence must have hung over the table as the prominent people nervously tried to hide their embarrassment. Jesus spoiled the party.

There is no room in Scripture for a one-sided view of our Lord. Jesus always oversteps the comfort zones of people. He hits the light switch in stuffy rooms of darkness and evil. He barges into our lives, tearing aside the curtains we've tried to pull over secret sins. He heaves His shoulder against the doors we've locked to protect private habits from His scrutiny.

Jesus always "talks out of turn," such as around banquet tables with prominent guests of honor. Always, always He urges some inconvenient, untimely change in people's lives. And how are we to respond? "He who humbles himself will be exalted."

JONI EARECKSON TADA

LEARNING HUMILITY

LUKE 14:11 NLT
"For the proud will be humbled,
but the humble will be honored."

People are hungry for the Word of God that will give peace, that will give unity, that will give joy. But you cannot give what you don't have. That's why it is necessary to deepen your life of prayer.

Be sincere in your prayers. Sincerity is humility, and you acquire humility only by accepting humiliations. All that has been said about humility is not enough to teach you humility. All that you have read about humility is not enough to teach you humility. You learn humility only by accepting humiliations. And you will meet humiliation all through your life. The greatest humiliation is to know that you are nothing. This you come to know when you face God in prayer.

Often a deep and fervent look at Christ is the best prayer: I look at Him and He looks at me. When you come face to face with God, you cannot but know that you are nothing, that you have nothing.

MOTHER TERESA

THE CALL TO HUMILITY

"Worthy are you, our Lord and God,
to receive glory and honor and power,
for you created all things,
and by your will they existed and were created."

The call to humility has been too little regarded in the Church, because its true nature and importance has been too little apprehended. It is not something which we bring to God, or He bestows; it is simply *the sense of entire nothingness, which comes when we see how truly God is all, and in which we make way for God to be all.* When the creature realises that this is the true nobility, and consents to be with his will, his mind, and his affections, the form, the vessel in which the life and glory of God are to work and manifest themselves, he sees that humility is simply acknowledging the truth of his position as creature, and yielding to God His place.

ANDREW MURRAY

GREATNESS THROUGH HUMILITY

PHILIPPIANS 2:8 NASB

Being found in appearance as a man,
He humbled Himself by becoming obedient
to the point of death, even death on a cross.

Jesus comes on the scene, and immediately we are made to realize that here is One that is great because of His humility. . . . One who could not get enthralled about the mighty and the noble, or share the enthusiasm of the disciples about the splendour of the Temple. But One who saw beauty in the "lily of the field." One who would not break the "bruised reed," or quench the "smoking flax."

. . . True greatness is always identified with humility and weakness and insignificance and lowliness. That is why the great and mighty God of the universe who created all things could not forever remain high and lifted up in the heavens—with a reputation of being mighty and powerful, but unconcerned about the needs of the people whom He created. He must come down and show Himself as He really is. For God the Father, living in His own Son in all His fullness, truly revealed Himself as He really is—meek, and lowly, and compassionate.

GEORGE WARNOCK

THE FRAGILITY OF HUMILITY

LUKE 18:9–12 NIV

To some who were confident of their own righteousness
and looked down on everybody else, Jesus told this
parable: "Two men went up to the temple to pray,
one a Pharisee and the other a tax collector.
The Pharisee stood up and prayed about himself:
'God, I thank you that I am not like other men—
robbers, evildoers, adulterers—or even like
this tax collector. I fast twice a week and
give a tenth of all I get.'"

Some years ago I saw what is called a sensitive plant. I happened to breathe on it, and suddenly it drooped its head; I touched it, and it withered away. Humility is as sensitive as that; it cannot safely be brought out on exhibition. A man who is flattering himself that he is humble and is walking close to the Master, is self-deceived. It consists not in thinking meanly of ourselves, but in not thinking of ourselves at all. Moses wist not that his face shone. If humility speaks of itself, it is gone.

D. L. MOODY

WHICH ONE ARE YOU?

LUKE 18:10–11 ESV

"Two men went up into the temple to pray,
one a Pharisee and the other a tax collector.
The Pharisee, standing by himself, prayed thus:
'God, I thank you that I am not like other men,
extortioners, unjust, adulterers, or
even like this tax collector.'"

Most of us would like to identify with the tax col- lector. But frankly, we may be more like the Pharisee—a good, solid citizen who does things above the religious call of duty and would never consider him- self capable of gross sinning.

Still convinced you are most like the repentant tax col- lector? Then try the test of the Lord's words from Luke 18. Are you confident of your own righteousness? Do you compare yourself with others to see if you're closer to the top? Do you, like the Pharisee, spend most of your prayer time petitioning God about yourself? If you an- swer yes to any of these questions, then it's time to swal- low the Lord's prescription: Humble yourself.

JONI EARECKSON TADA

DON'T ADMIRE YOURSELF

LUKE 18:11 NKJV

"The Pharisee stood and prayed thus with himself,
'God, I thank You that I am not like other men—
extortioners, unjust, adulterers, or
even as this tax collector.'"

In whatever you do for a fellow-servant, remember that your Master has done it to your servants. Listen and shudder! Never be pleased by your humility! . . . Have you done any act out of humility? Don't be proud of it, otherwise all its merit is lost. The Pharisee was like this. He was puffed up because he gave his tithes to the poor, and, as a result, he lost the honor of the deed. But not so with the tax collector. Nor with Paul who said, "I know nothing by myself, yet am I not hereby justified." See how he doesn't exalt himself, but in every way lowers and humbles himself, even when he had arrived at the summit. . . . When you think about admiring yourself because you are humble, consider your Master. Remember what He descended into and you won't admire or praise yourself anymore.

JOHN CHRYSOSTOM

BE REAL

LUKE 18:11–12 NCV

*"The Pharisee stood alone and prayed, 'God, I thank
you that I am not like other people who steal,
cheat, or take part in adultery, or even like this
tax collector. I give up eating twice a week,
and I give one-tenth of everything I get!'"*

If the Bible is about anything at all, it is about God having mercy on the pitiful plight of men, forgiving their
sins and restoring their lives. Christ never resisted the
truly repentant, but the Pharisees on the other hand could
really get to Him.

. . . You don't want to be like the Pharisees. Better to
admit where you're not and ask God's help to get you
where you need to be. Do not fake a manifestation of the
Spirit that isn't there. Have no confidence in your flesh.
Just be real before Him. That's what He wants from you.
That's what He wants from all of us.

. . . The way home is humility. Make no excuses. Ra-
tionalize nothing. Blame no one. Humble yourself. If you
don't yet feel the sorrow that you know will be necessary,
ask Him for it like a beggar asks for bread.

BETH MOORE

THE NEED FOR HUMILITY

———

LUKE 18:11–13 NIV

*"The Pharisee stood up and prayed about himself:
'God, I thank you that I am not like other men—
robbers, evildoers, adulterers—or even like this
tax collector. I fast twice a week and give a tenth
of all I get.' But the tax collector stood
at a distance. He would not even look up
to heaven, but beat his breast and said,
'God, have mercy on me, a sinner.'"*

There are two realms in which humility is of supreme importance. It is important in the realm of knowledge. No man will ever begin to learn unless he realizes that he does not know; therefore the first prerequisite of learning is the admission of one's ignorance. Again, humility is of supreme importance in the realm of the spirit. It has been said that the gateway to heaven is so low that no one can enter except upon his knees. The first essential of all religion is a sense of need. The man who is proudly self-sufficient cannot find God; the man who is humble enough to know his need will find the way open to His presence.

WILLIAM BARCLAY

THE TAX COLLECTOR

LUKE 18:13–14 NASB

"But the tax collector, standing some distance away,
was even unwilling to lift up his eyes to heaven,
but was beating his breast, saying, 'God, be merciful
to me, the sinner!' I tell you, this man went
to his house justified rather than the other;
for everyone who exalts himself will be humbled,
but he who humbles himself will be exalted."

God be merciful to me a sinner." Here is no confidence in the flesh, no plea fetched from fasting, paying tithes, or the performance of any other duty; here is no boasting that he was not an extortioner, unjust, or an adulterer. Perhaps he had been guilty of all these crimes, at least he knew he would have been guilty of all these, had he been left to follow the devices and desires of his own heart; and therefore, with a broken and contrite spirit, he cries out, "God be merciful to me a sinner."

This man came up to the temple to pray, and he prayed indeed. And a broken and contrite heart God will not despise. "I tell you," says our Lord, . . . "this man," this Publican, this despised, sinful, but broken-hearted man, "went down to his house justified (acquitted, and looked upon as righteous in the sight of God) rather than the other."

GEORGE WHITEFIELD

THE MEANING OF HUMILITY

LUKE 18:13 NKJV

"And the tax collector, standing afar off, would not so much as raise his eyes to heaven, but beat his breast, saying, 'God, be merciful to me a sinner!'"

What is the opposite of this pride that kills sympathy and empathy and other-oriented joy and other-oriented sorrow? The opposite can be described in two ways. One, of course, is to call it *humility*. Humility would be not thinking of ourselves all the time. It would be not being infatuated with ourselves, but finding others interesting and even superior in many ways. Humility would be not exalting ourselves but loving to exalt others. That's one way to describe the opposite of pride.

But there is a problem with that description of the alternative to pride. There's no God in it. There's no Christ in it. Strictly speaking, this humility is atheistic. The biblical, Christian alternative to pride is not natural humility, but *faith in Jesus Christ,* the creator and redeemer of the universe. The Christian alternative to self-preoccupation and self-infatuation and self-exaltation is Christ-preoccupation and Christ-infatuation and Christ-exaltation. The Christian alternative to thinking of ourselves more highly than we ought to is faith—that is, turning away from self to Christ.

JOHN PIPER

OUR ONLY DELIVERANCE

LUKE 18:13 KJV

And the publican, standing afar off, would not lift up
so much as his eyes unto heaven, but smote upon
his breast, saying, God be merciful to me a sinner.

I n this confession, he implicitly acknowledgeth, that sin
is the worst of things, forasmuch as it layeth the soul
without the reach of all remedy that can be found under
heaven. Nothing below, or short of the mercy of God,
can deliver a poor soul from this fearful malady. This the
Pharisee did not see. Doubtless he did conclude, that at
some time or other he had sinned; but he never in all his
life did arrive to a sight of what sin was. . . . But the poor
Publican he had it, he had it in truth, as is manifest,
because it drives him to the only sovereign remedy. For
indeed, the right knowledge of sin, in the guilt and filth,
and damning power thereof, makes a man to understand,
that not any thing but grace and mercy by Christ, can
secure him from the hellish ruins thereof.

JOHN BUNYAN

BECOMING LIKE CHILDREN

LUKE 18:13–14 ESV

"But the tax collector, standing far off, would not even lift up his eyes to heaven, but beat his breast, saying, 'God, be merciful to me, a sinner!' I tell you, this man went down to his house justified, rather than the other. For everyone who exalts himself will be humbled, but the one who humbles himself will be exalted."

While the disciples were arguing about who was most important, our Lord, the teacher of humility, took a little child and said: "Except ye be converted and become as little children ye cannot enter the kingdom of heaven." And, lest it appear that He preached more than He practiced, Christ fulfilled His own command. For He washed His disciples' feet. He received the traitor with a kiss. He spoke with the Samaritan woman. He talked about the kingdom of heaven with Mary at His feet. And when He rose again from the dead, He showed Himself to some poor women first. Pride is opposed to humility, and through it Satan lost his high position as an archangel. . . . As Scripture says: "God resisteth the proud and giveth grace to the humble." Beloved, think what a great sin it must be to have God as its opponent. For in the Gospels, the Pharisee is rejected because of his pride but the publican is accepted because of his humility.

JEROME

HUMILITY AND GRACE

LUKE 18:14 NIV

"I tell you that this man, rather than the other, went home justified before God. For everyone who exalts himself will be humbled, and he who humbles himself will be exalted."

I fear that there are not a few who, by strong expressions of self-condemnation and self-denunciation, have sought to humble themselves, and have to confess with sorrow that a humble spirit, a 'heart of humility,' with its accompaniments of kindness and compassion, of meekness and forbearance, is still as far off as ever. Being occupied with self, even amid the deepest self-abhorrence, can never free us from self. It is the revelation of God, not only by the law condemning sin, but by His grace delivering from it, that will make us humble. The law may break the heart with fear; it is only grace that works that sweet humility which becomes a joy to the soul as its second nature. It was the revelation of God in His holiness, drawing nigh to make Himself known in His grace, that made Abraham and Jacob, Job and Isaiah, bow so low.

ANDREW MURRAY

THE BLINDNESS OF HYPOCRISY

LUKE 18:14 KJV

I tell you, this man went down to his house justified rather than the other: for every one that exalteth himself shall be abased; and he that humbleth himself shall be exalted.

Now let us better see and hear what the Lord says to this. There stands the publican and humbles himself, says nothing of fasting, nothing of his good works, nor of anything. Yet the Lord says that his sins are not so great as the sins of the hypocrite; even in spite of anyone now exalting himself above the lowest sinner. If I exalt myself a finger's breadth above my neighbor, or the vilest sinner, then am I cast down. For the publican during his whole life did not do as many and as great sins as this Pharisee does here when he says: I thank thee God, that I am not as other men are; and lies enough to burst all heaven. . . . The public gross sins that break out are insignificant; but unbelief which is in the heart and we cannot see, this is the real sin.

MARTIN LUTHER

POSITION AND PRIDE

1 CORINTHIANS 4:7 NIV
For who makes you different from anyone else?
What do you have that you did not receive?
And if you did receive it, why do you boast
as though you did not?

B ut what is important is that you rightly understand
what Christ means by these words and realize that, if
you are of a higher rank or are in some way above others,
this is something that has been given to you by God, but
not in order that you may put on airs on account of this
gift and ride roughshod over everybody else, as if you
were better than others in the sight of God because of it.
On the contrary, he has commanded that you be humble
and serve your neighbor with it. . . . Thus he made others princes, lords, noblemen, regents, scholars and to this
end gave them sovereignty, power, honor, great understanding, etc. . . . But most of them sin by their pride and
arrogance, especially in these days when there is altogether too much insolence and presumption among the
upper classes and also gross peasant's pride among others.

MARTIN LUTHER

THE DELIGHT OF HUMILITY

JAMES 4:10 ESV
*Humble yourselves before the Lord,
and he will exalt you.*

The point is, He wants you to know Him: wants to give you Himself. And He and you are two things of such a kind that if you really get into any kind of touch with Him you will, in fact, be humble—delightedly humble, feeling the infinite relief of having for once got rid of all the silly nonsense about your own dignity which has made you restless and unhappy all your life. He is trying to make you humble in order to make this moment possible: trying to take off a lot of silly, ugly, fancy-dress in which we have all got ourselves up and are strutting about like the little idiots we are. I wish I had got a bit further with humility myself: if I had, I could probably tell you more about the relief, the comfort. . . . To get even near it, even for a moment, is like a drink of cold water to a man in a desert.

C. S. LEWIS

BOASTING IN WEAKNESS

2 CORINTHIANS 12:9 NIV
*But he said to me, "My grace is sufficient for you,
for my power is made perfect in weakness."
Therefore I will boast all the more gladly
about my weaknesses, so that Christ's
power may rest on me.*

A clearer insight was given to Paul into the deep truth that the presence of Christ will banish every desire to seek anything in ourselves, and will make us delight in every humiliation that prepares us for His fuller manifestation. Our humiliations lead us, in the experience of the presence and power of Jesus Christ, to choose humility as our highest blessing. . . .

There may be advanced believers, eminent teachers, people of heavenly experiences, who have not yet fully learned the lesson of perfect humility, of gladly glorying in weakness. We see this in Paul. He was dangerously close to exalting himself. He didn't yet know perfectly what it was to be nothing, to die that Christ alone might live in him, and to take pleasure in all that brought him low. It appears as if this were the highest lesson he had to learn—full conformity to his Lord in that self-emptying where he gloried in weakness so Christ might be all.

ANDREW MURRAY

OWN YOUR FAULTS

1 PETER 5:5 NKJV
Yes, all of you be submissive to one another,
and be clothed with humility, for
"God resists the proud,
But gives grace to the humble."

We often think that we have no need of anyone else's advice or reproof. Always remember, much grace does not imply much enlightenment. We may be wise but have little love, or we may have love with little wisdom. God has wisely joined us all together as the parts of a body so that we cannot say to another, "I have no need of you."

. . . Let there be in you that lowly mind which was in Christ Jesus. Be clothed with humility. Let modesty appear in all your words and actions.

One way we do this is to own any fault we have. If you have at any time thought, spoken, or acted wrong, do not refrain from acknowledging it. Never dream that this will hurt the cause of God—in fact, it will further it. Be open and honest when you are rebuked and do not seek to evade it or disguise it. Rather, let it appear just as it is and you will thereby not hinder but adorn the gospel.

JOHN WESLEY

GREATNESS THROUGH SERVANTHOOD

1 PETER 5:6 NCV
*Be humble under God's powerful hand so he
will lift you up when the right time comes.*

We serve as a stepping-stone to greatness, but serving itself is greatness; it is being like Christ. Ironically, if you want to rule with Christ, don't try to seek this reward by finding a lofty position and using it as a stepping-stone to something greater. Find a towel, a basin, and some dirty feet and take the role of a servant. Within God's good time, He may see fit to give you greater responsibility. "Humble yourselves, therefore, under the mighty hand of God, that He may exalt you at the proper time" (1 Peter 5:6). To want exaltation is fair enough, but it can only be achieved through humility. Paradoxically, *the very thing we seek, greatness, is found through its opposite, humility!*

If we wish to be great in the kingdom, we must begin by serving our spouses, our children, and any needy person we can help. We must die to our natural desire to be served and begin to serve, taking the initiative in meeting the needs of others.

ERWIN W. LUTZER

HUMBLE SERVICE

HEBREWS 13:16 NKJV
*But do not forget to do good and to share, for
with such sacrifices God is well pleased.*

Be humble and innocent, and you will be like the children who don't know the wickedness that ruins men's lives. First, then, speak evil of no one, nor listen with pleasure to anyone who speaks evil of another. But if you listen and believe the slander which you hear, you will participate in the sin of him who speaks evil. . . . Keep yourself from it, and you will always be at peace with everyone. Put on a holiness that will not offend with wickedness, but whose actions are all steady and joyful. Practice goodness; and from your profit, . . . give to all, for God wants His gifts to be shared among everyone. . . . This service, then, if completed in humility, is glorious to God. He, therefore, who ministers with humility, will live to God. Therefore keep these commandments as I have given them to you so that your repentance and the repentance of your house may be found innocent and your heart may be pure and stainless.

HERMAS

PICTURES OF
MONEY

"No one can serve two masters.
Either he will hate the one and
love the other, or he will be devoted
to the one and despise the other.
You cannot serve both God and Money."
MATTHEW 6:24 NIV

PICTURES OF MONEY

It comes as little surprise that Jesus gave a lot of attention to the chief competition against God for our affections—money and possessions. Several of his parables vividly portray the life-and-death struggle between our love for God and our love for the things of this world. Ultimately, Jesus points out, we cannot serve both. Either God or "mammon" will secure our final allegiance. Earthly treasure turns out to be a cruel ally in victory—it stays behind when we die. With God, we have everything worth having; without God, we end up with nothing.

It turns out that humans have had materialistic tendencies for a long time! Jesus' parables about money and possessions sound like they could have been told today. Examine the struggle in your experiences as you read the selections in this section. You may discover your life is actually a battlefield and you have been fighting for the wrong side.

Treasure on Earth

Matthew 6:19 NKJV

"Do not lay up for yourselves treasures on earth,
where moth and rust destroy
and where thieves break in and steal."

It is human and natural to want to lay up treasure, so Jesus tells his disciples, "Lay up for yourselves treasures in heaven," not on earth. Why should we not lay up treasure on earth? For three reasons.

First, laying up treasure on earth is *daft* because in the long run such treasure is of very little value. You can't keep it (moth and rust consume it), nor take it with you (think of the rich fool, Luke 12:16–21). . . .

Second, laying up treasure on earth is *dangerous* because such treasure destroys spiritual awareness. . . . If your heart is possessed by what this world and this life offer, you will not be able to see spiritual issues clearly, and when you read the Bible, its full meaning will escape you.

Third, laying up treasure on earth is *disastrous* because no one can serve two masters. . . . And to have God pass the verdict that one has not served him is life's ultimate disaster.

J. I. Packer

LONGING

MATTHEW 6:20 NRSV
*"Store up for yourselves treasures in heaven,
where neither moth nor rust consumes and
where thieves do not break in and steal."*

Most people, if they had really learned to look into their own hearts, would know that they do want, and want acutely, something that cannot be had in this world. There are all sorts of things in this world that offer to give it to you, but they never quite keep their promise. The longings which arise in us when we first fall in love, or first think of some foreign country, or first take up some subject that excites us, are longings which no marriage, no travel, no learning, can really satisfy. I am not now speaking of what would ordinarily be called unsuccessful marriages, or holidays, or learned careers. I am speaking of the best possible ones. There was something we grasped at, in that first moment of longing, which just fades away in reality. I think everyone knows what I mean. The wife may be a good wife, and the hotels and scenery may have been excellent, and chemistry may be a very interesting job: but something has evaded us.

C. S. LEWIS

THE HEART'S TREASURE

MATTHEW 6:21 NIV
*"For where your treasure is,
there your heart will be also."*

J esus concludes this first saying about money: "Where your treasure is, there shall your heart be." What a person treasures reveals everything about that person's heart, because the heart is the center for making decisions. Jonathan Swift wisely commented that it is one thing to have money on your mind; it is another to have money in your heart. From Jesus' perspective, earthly treasure is a snare because it causes us to give our hearts to this transient, material world. We can become consumed with the consumption of things, things that are here today and gone tomorrow. They can easily slip through our fingers, so we become absorbed by concerns for their security. The result is that we cannot be pure-hearted, focused entirely upon God. And when our heart is not directed toward God, we are at risk of losing everything.

DAVID S. DOCKERY

DARKNESS AND LIGHT

MATTHEW 6:22–23 NLT

*"Your eye is a lamp for your body. A pure eye lets
sunshine into your soul. But an evil eye shuts out
the light and plunges you into darkness.
If the light you think you have is really darkness,
how deep that darkness will be!"*

Worldly possessions tend to turn the hearts of the disciples away from Jesus. What are we really devoted to? That is the question. Are our hearts set on earthly goods? Do we try to combine devotion to them with loyalty to Christ? Or are we devoted exclusively to him? The light of the body is the eye, and the light of the Christian is his heart. If the eye be dark, how great is the darkness of the body! But the heart is dark when it clings to earthly goods, for then, however urgently Jesus may call us, his call fails to find access to our hearts. Our hearts are closed, for they have already been given to another. As the light cannot penetrate the body when the eye is evil, so the word of Jesus cannot penetrate the disciple's heart so long as it is closed against it. The word is choked like the seed which was sown among thorns, choked "with cares and riches and pleasures of this life" (Luke 8:14).

DIETRICH BONHOEFFER

A LIFE OF GLADNESS

MATTHEW 6:24 NASB

*"No one can serve two masters; for either he will hate the
one and love the other, or he will be devoted to one and
despise the other. You cannot serve God and wealth."*

Those who are God's are always glad, when they are
not divided, because they only want what God
wants, and want to do for him all that he wishes. They
divest themselves of everything, and in this divesting find
a hundredfold return. Peace of conscience, liberty of
heart, the sweetness of abandoning ourselves in the hands
of God, the joy of always seeing the light grow in our
hearts, finally, freedom from the fears and insatiable desires
of the times, multiply a hundredfold the happiness which
the true children of God possess in the midst of their
crosses, if they are faithful.

They sacrifice themselves, but to what they love most.
They suffer, but they want to suffer, and they prefer the
suffering to every false joy. Their bodies endure sharp
pain, their imagination is troubled, their spirit droops in
weakness and exhaustion, but their will is firm and quiet
in their deepest and most intimate self, and it constantly
says, "Amen," to all the blows with which God strikes it
to sacrifice it.

FRANÇOIS FÉNELON

SERVING TWO MASTERS

MATTHEW 6:24 ESV
*"No one can serve two masters, for either he will
hate the one and love the other, or he will be
devoted to the one and despise the other.
You cannot serve God and money."*

Some people disagree with this saying of Jesus. . . .
They blandly assure us that it is perfectly possible to
serve two masters simultaneously, for they manage it very
nicely themselves. Several possible arrangements and
adjustments appeal to them. Either they serve God on
Sundays and mammon on weekdays, or God with their
lips and mammon with their hearts, or God in appearance
and mammon in reality, or God with half their being and
mammon with the other half.

. . . Would-be compromisers misunderstand His teaching, for they miss the picture of slave and slave-owner
which lies behind his words. As [A. H.] McNeile puts it,
'Men can work for two employers, but no slave can be the
property of two owners,' for 'single ownership and full-
time service are of the essence of slavery.' So anybody
who divides his allegiance between God and mammon
has already given it to mammon, since God can be served
only with an entire and exclusive devotion.

JOHN R. W. STOTT

TRANSFER YOUR TREASURE

LUKE 12:33–34 NIV

"Sell your possessions and give to the poor.
Provide purses for yourselves that will not wear out,
a treasure in heaven that will not be exhausted,
where no thief comes near and no moth destroys. For
where your treasure is, there your heart will be also."

L et experience correct the man whom words do not
correct. There will be no arousing or advance unless
we all cry out with one voice: 'Woe to us! The world is
falling.' If it is falling, why do you not forsake it? If an
architect were to tell you that your house was about to
crumble, would you not quit it before you began to com-
plain? But the Builder of the world tells you that the
world will crumble. Do you not believe Him? Hear
His forewarning voice; heed His words of admonition.
His forewarning voice is this: 'Heaven and earth will pass
away.' These are His words of admonition: 'Do not lay up
for yourselves treasure on earth.' . . . Then I give this
advice: 'Give to the poor, and thou shalt have treasure in
heaven.' You will not remain without treasure, but what
you possess on earth with anxiety you shall have with
security in heaven. Therefore, transport your possessions.
My advice is for preservation, not for loss.

AUGUSTINE

FAITH AND WORLDLY WISDOM

HEBREWS 11:24, 26 NIV
*By faith Moses, when he had grown up, refused
to be known as the son of Pharaoh's daughter. . . .
He regarded disgrace for the sake of Christ
as of greater value than the treasures of Egypt,
because he was looking ahead to his reward.*

Faith is the refusal of the small, for the sake of the large.
Faith will make no decision, take no step, merely
from worldly motives; for it sees past the immediate good
to a richer, grander good. Worldly-wisdom is not wisdom; it is folly, the blind grasping at what is within reach.
It is folly, for any present good, to cut yourself off from
your true life. A good conscience, peace of heart, faith,
the vision of God, the hope of glory—it is a fool's bar-
gain . . . to barter these for any mess of pottage. To rake
in the dust-heap for scraps of treasure heedless of the
golden crown to be had for the looking and the taking—
that was Lot's choice, and that is the choice of every soul
who seeks *first* the world.

HUGH BLACK

A QUESTION OF PRIORITIES

*The young man said to him, "I have kept all these;
what do I still lack?" Jesus said to him, "If you wish
to be perfect, go, sell your possessions, and give
the money to the poor, and you will have treasure
in heaven; then come, follow me."*

Was this then Jesus' formula, the renunciation of private possessions, a sharing out of wealth, an egalitarian society? If this story were all the evidence we had, we might well think so. But it is not. Some of Jesus' followers were, and remained, rich and influential men. Jesus' very dependence on hospitality demanded that some of his supporters kept their homes and their jobs. Even Peter, a constant member of Jesus' closest entourage, seems to have kept both his home and his boat and fishing gear. . . .

Then why did Jesus make this staggering demand of this one would-be disciple? His remarks after the man had gone do not suggest that he demanded poverty or renunciation for their own sake, but that it was a question of priorities. It is not necessarily wrong to be rich, but it can be dangerous. Money has a way of taking control of its owner, and it makes a tyrannous master; it can stop a man following the call of God.

R. T. FRANCE

BARRIERS TO THE KINGDOM

MATTHEW 19:21 NLT

Jesus told him, "If you want to be perfect, go and
sell all you have and give the money to the poor,
and you will have treasure in heaven.
Then come, follow me."

Jesus said something to this young man he is never recorded to have said to another. He looked into his heart and saw what was holding him back from making this decision. The young man was rich; and Jesus perceived that he was attached to his wealth. Therefore Jesus said, "Your decision for the Kingdom of God must be unqualified. Your wealth is standing in your way. Therefore, go and sell everything you have, and you will then be free to follow me."

It should be clear that liquidation of wealth of itself would not make this young man a disciple. Discipleship, decision was lodged in the demand, "Follow me." The man could have become a pauper and still have remained outside the Kingdom had he not followed Jesus. Disposition of wealth was not itself discipleship; but in this case it was a necessary prelude to discipleship. Jesus demanded the removal of a barrier. Anything, whether wealth or career or family, which stands in the way of decision must yield before the claims of God's Kingdom.

GEORGE ELDON LADD

THE RICH AND THE POOR

LUKE 12:16–17 NKJV
Then He spoke a parable to them, saying:
"The ground of a certain rich man yielded plentifully.
And he thought within himself, saying, 'What shall
I do, since I have no room to store my crops?'"

I t is evident that none of these rich men—the one of
this parable, the young man who asked what he still
lacked to inherit eternal life, and the other one at whose
gate Lazarus was laid—considered his wealth a gift from
God. If they had, they would have understood that they
were stewards of God's gift rather than possessors. In this
way, the rich man can "be rich toward God" and not simply "lay up treasures" for himself (Luke 12:21). . . .

Greed, the insatiable desire to possess more, and covetousness, envy of others for what they possess, are not,
however, exclusively sins of the rich. A person of rela-
tively modest means can be just as guilty of these faults,
especially of covetousness. Some may even be filled with
anger and resentment for not having what they consider
their due. Worse yet, they may blame *God* for their poverty. In the final analysis, we all, rich and poor, must be
wise stewards of whatever we have.

ARCHBISHOP DMITRI

STORING OUR SURPLUS

LUKE 12:18–19 NIV

"Then he said, 'This is what I'll do. I will tear down
my barns and build bigger ones, and there I will store
all my grain and my goods. And I'll say to myself,
"You have plenty of good things laid up for many years.
Take life easy; eat, drink and be merry."'"

The rich man was a fool because he failed to realize
his dependence on others. . . . He talked as though
he could plow the fields and build the barns alone. He
failed to realize that he was an heir of a vast treasury of
ideas and labor to which both the living and the dead had
contributed. When an individual or a nation overlooks
this interdependence, we find a tragic foolishness.

We can clearly see the meaning of this parable for the
present world crisis. Our nation's productive machinery
constantly brings forth such an abundance of food that we
must build larger barns and spend more than a million
dollars daily to store our surplus. . . . What can we do?
The answer is simple: . . . We can store our surplus food
free of charge in the shriveled stomachs of the millions of
God's children who go to bed hungry at night. We can
use our vast resources of wealth to wipe poverty from the
earth.

MARTIN LUTHER KING, JR.

BEING RICH TOWARD GOD

LUKE 12:20–21 ESV
"But God said to him, 'Fool! This night your soul is required of you, and the things you have prepared, whose will they be?' So is the one who lays up treasure for himself and is not rich toward God."

We will never persuade our people that the parable of the rich fool (Luke 12:13–21) applies to them unless we apply it to ourselves. God called the man a fool because, when his fields produced a surplus, he built bigger barns and took his ease.

What should he have done with the God-given surplus? Verse 33 answers: "Sell your possessions, and give to the needy." Instead of increasing his own ease and security, he should have used his extra possessions to alleviate suffering. . . .

Being "rich toward God" means looking Godward for heavenly wealth. It means "taking your ease" in Him, finding your security in Him. And it means using your money in a way that enlarges the barn of your joy in heaven, not the barn of your comfort on earth. God gives us money on earth in order that we may invest it for dividends in heaven.

JOHN PIPER

THE UNCERTAINTY OF LIFE

LUKE 12:20–21 NRSV

"But God said to him, 'You fool! This very night your life is being demanded of you. And the things you have prepared, whose will they be?' So it is with those who store up treasures for themselves but are not rich toward God."

A man's life is an uncertain thing at best and no one has the assurance that he will live the years he would like. The really stupid thing was the rich man's easy assurance that the future was in his control. God said to him *This night . . . your soul is required of you.* The verb is literally 'they require,' a construction common among the rabbis to denote an action of God, i.e., 'God requires your soul.' A man whose life hangs by a thread and who may be called upon at any time to give account of himself is a fool if he relies on material things.

. . . Jesus rounds this off with a contrast between laying up treasure for oneself and being *rich toward God* (i.e., rich 'where God is concerned'). It is the latter that matters. People are fools to settle for less.

LEON MORRIS

WORLDLY SUCCESS

LUKE 6:24 NLT
*"What sorrows await you who are rich,
for you have your only happiness now."*

Jesus was too honest to pretend that the consolations of riches cannot be very real and very sweet, just as the pains of poverty can be very real and very bitter. But was the rich man to be congratulated on that account? Not for a moment. . . .

We say, "Woe! to the rich," but only because in our hearts we think them happy, happier than they deserve! How different the attitude of Jesus! Here again, His amazing originality and purity appear. He stands quite clear of all these fallacies and self-deceptions. To Him the success of the worldly is not an undeserved reward; on the contrary, it is their most terrible punishment, their entirely appropriate doom. He does not envy them it; He pities them rather. He says "woe to them," because He really thinks it is a most dreadful thing to aim at worldly success and get it. It would have been better for them to have aimed at it and *not* got it.

HERBERT HENRY FARMER

THE DANGER OF RICHES

1 TIMOTHY 6:9 NIV
*People who want to get rich fall into temptation and
a trap and into many foolish and harmful desires
that plunge men into ruin and destruction.*

Jesus teaches us not only that riches are to be despised,
but that also they are full of danger. They are the root
of seducing evils and deceive the blind human mind by
hidden deception. God rebukes rich fools who think only
of their earthly wealth and boast in the abundance of their
overflowing harvests. He says, "Thou fool, this night thy
soul shall be required of thee; then whose shall those
things be which thou hast provided?" The fool was
rejoicing in his supplies when he would die that very
night; one whose life was already failing was thinking
about the abundance of his food. However, the Lord tells
us that those who sell all their possessions and distribute
them for the poor become perfect and complete. In so
doing, they lay up treasures for themselves in heaven. He
says that those who follow Him . . . and aren't entangled
by worldly possessions . . . accompany their possessions
which they send to God. For such a reward, let us all prepare ourselves.

CYPRIAN

THE MISERY OF GREED

---

1 TIMOTHY 6:9 NLT

*But people who long to be rich fall into temptation and
are trapped by many foolish and harmful desires
that plunge them into ruin and destruction.*

Think of the misery that comes into our lives by our
restless gnawing greed. We plunge ourselves into
enormous debt and then take two and three jobs to stay
afloat. We uproot our families with unnecessary moves
just so we can have a more prestigious house. We grasp
and grab and never have enough. And most destructive
of all, our flashy cars and sports spectaculars and backyard
pools have a way of crowding out much interest in civil
rights or inner city poverty or the starved masses of India.
Greed has a way of severing the cords of compassion.
How clearly the Apostle Paul saw this when he warned
that our lust for wealth causes us to fall into "many sense-
less and hurtful desires that plunge men into ruin and
destruction" (I Timothy 6:9).

But we do not need to be imprisoned to avarice. We
can be ushered into a life of peace and serenity. With Paul
we can say, "If we have food and clothing, with these we
shall be content" (6:8).

RICHARD J. FOSTER

FAITHFUL IN LITTLE THINGS

1 CORINTHIANS 4:2 NASB
*In this case, moreover, it is required of stewards
that one be found trustworthy.*

Too many people are not faithful in little things. They are not to be absolutely depended upon. They do not always keep their promises. They break engagements. They fail to pay their debts promptly. They come behind time to appointments. They are neglectful and careless in little things. In general they are good people, but their life is honeycombed with small failures. One who can be positively depended upon, who is faithful in the least things as well as in the greatest, whose life and character are true through and through, gives out a light in this world which honors Christ and blesses others.

J. R. MILLER

WORDS TO THE WEALTHY

REVELATION 3:20 NKJV
"Behold, I stand at the door and knock.
If anyone hears My voice and opens the door,
I will come in to him and dine with him,
and he with Me."

Therefore, don't let the wealthy consider themselves excluded from the Savior's lists at the outset, provided they are believers and contemplate the greatness of God's generosity. Don't let them expect to gain the crowns of eternal life without struggle and effort, training or challenge. Instead, let them put themselves under the Word as their trainer and Christ as the official of the contest. For their prescribed food and drink, let them have the New Testament of the Lord; for exercises, the commandments; and for elegance and adornment, the beauty of love, faith, hope, knowledge of the truth, gentleness, humility, compassion, and dignity. Then, when the last trumpet signals the race and departure from the stadium of life, they may, with good consciences, present themselves victorious to the Judge who gives the rewards. They will be worthy of their heavenly Fatherland, to which they will return with crowns and the praise of angels.

CLEMENT OF ALEXANDRIA

FAITH AND GOOD DEEDS

LUKE 16:1–2 NIV

*Jesus told his disciples: "There was a rich man whose
manager was accused of wasting his possessions.
So he called him in and asked him, 'What is this
I hear about you? Give an account of your management, because you cannot be manager any longer.'"*

Make to yourselves friends by means of the mammon of unrighteousness; that, when it shall fail,
they may receive you into the eternal tabernacles." You
say, our adversaries cry: you say a person shall not do good
works to obtain eternal life; behold, here it reads differently. Now, what shall we answer? . . . If we wish to enter
into judgment before God with our good works, we cast
Christ aside as our Mediator, and cannot stand before
God. Therefore let him remain our Mediator and abide
thou under the shadow of his wings. . . .

You must hence remember that eternal life consists of
two things, faith and what follows faith. If you go and
believe and do good to your neighbor, everlasting life
must follow, although you never think about it. Just as
when you take a good drink, the taste will follow as soon
as you drink, even though you do not seek it.

MARTIN LUTHER

SHREWDNESS

LUKE 16:3-6 NIV

"The manager said to himself, 'What shall I do now?
My master is taking away my job. I'm not strong
enough to dig, and I'm ashamed to beg—I know what
I'll do so that, when I lose my job here, people will
welcome me into their houses.' So he called in each one
of his master's debtors. He asked the first, 'How much
do you owe my master?' 'Eight hundred gallons of olive
oil,' he replied. The manager told him, 'Take your bill,
sit down quickly, and make it four hundred.'"

Men and women whose outlook on life is conditioned by the Dow are shrewder on the street than are the disciples on their spiritual journey. Unbelievers put us to shame. Imitate their shrewdness!

Jesus did not excuse the steward's action but admired his initiative. He did not let a tragic sequence of events unfold but did what he had to do, however unscrupulously, to make a new life for himself. Without illusions, he makes the most of the little time that remains.

BRENNAN MANNING

LESSONS FROM A DISHONEST STEWARD

LUKE 16:8–9 NRSV

"And his master commended the dishonest manager
because he had acted shrewdly; for the children of
this age are more shrewd in dealing with their
own generation than are the children of light.
And I tell you, make friends for yourselves by means
of dishonest wealth so that when it is gone,
they may welcome you into the eternal homes."

A crisis does not make a man but it shows what a man is made of. The Lord Jesus did not commend this steward for his unethical actions. He commended him for his wise use of his opportunities ... They are not wiser when it comes to spiritual things, and their wisdom extends only to their generation and not to eternity. But we can learn from this dishonest employee how to make the most of our opportunities. ...

The steward made some radical changes in his life when he realized he was going to face his master and give account. He started using present opportunities for future blessings. He started living for people and not for things, for investment and not for mere enjoyment.

... If we use our material possessions wisely today, we will enjoy them more, and we will have friends in heaven who came to know Christ because we were faithful stewards.

WARREN W. WIERSBE

WISDOM FROM THE WORLD

LUKE 16:8–9 ESV

"The master commended the dishonest manager for his
shrewdness. For the sons of this world are more shrewd
in dealing with their own generation than the sons of
light. And I tell you, make friends for yourselves by
means of unrighteous wealth, so that when it fails
they may receive you into the eternal dwellings."

Thus he compares here the unjust to the just. As the unjust man acts shrewdly, though wrongly and like a rogue, so we also should act shrewdly but righteously in godliness. This is the proper understanding of this parable. For the Lord says: "The children of this world are wiser than the children of light." So that the children of light should learn wisdom from the children of darkness or the world. Just as they are wise in their transactions, so should also the children of light be wise in their transactions. . . .

Luke has described the fruit of faith thus: Give to the poor and make to yourself friends. As though he would say: I will not now speak of faith, but how you should prove your faith. Wherefore do good to your neighbor, and if you can give from the heart you may be assured that you believe.

MARTIN LUTHER

PLEASING GOD

LUKE 16:10 NRSV
*"Whoever is faithful in a very little is faithful also
in much; and whoever is dishonest in a very
little is dishonest also in much."*

But the most dangerous thing is that the soul, by the neglect of little things, becomes accustomed to unfaithfulness. It saddens the Holy Spirit; it yields to its own impulses; it makes nothing of failing God. On the contrary, true love sees nothing as little. Everything which can please or displease God always seems great to it. It is not that true love throws the soul into fussing and scruples, but it does place no limits to its fidelity. It acts simply with God, and as it is quite untroubled by the things which God does not ask of it, it also never wants to hesitate a single instant in that which God does ask of it. Thus, it is not by fussiness that we become faithful and exact in the smallest things. It is by a feeling of love, which is free from the reflections and fears of the anxious and scrupulous.

FRANÇOIS FÉNELON

THE TRAP OF WEALTH

1 TIMOTHY 6:9–10 NIV
People who want to get rich fall into temptation and
a trap and into many foolish and harmful desires that
plunge men into ruin and destruction. For the love
of money is a root of all kinds of evil.

A person who is weak in spirit and who is still controlled by his *need* to be important has great trouble
dragging himself away from the things that most attract
him in this world. Such a person is unhappy when he
does restrain himself, yet his anger flares up if anyone
stands in his way. What is more, if he does get what he
wants, he is at once stricken by a heavy conscience
because he has given in to his weakness. In no way does
this lead to peace!

In resisting such temptations, then, does one find true
peace of heart, not in being a slave to them. There is no
peace in the heart of a slave, nor in someone who is
driven to continually bustling about in the world. Only a
spiritual person—a person aglow with God's love—finds
true peace.

THOMAS À KEMPIS

THE IDOL OF MONEY

ECCLESIASTES 5:10 ESV
He who loves money will not be satisfied with money,
nor he who loves wealth with his income;
this also is vanity.

As we become exposed to the poor and their needs, the rich young ruler and the widow and her mite lose the storybook quality of our childhood faith, and become figures in the counter-culture literature of a revolutionary leader—the very one whom we call Saviour. . . . Some of us have looked into the face of our idols and found that one of them is money.

Though we along with millions of other churchgoers are saying that Jesus saves, we ask ourselves if we are not in practice acting as though it were money that saves. We say that money gives power, money corrupts, money talks. Like the ancients with their molten calf we have endowed money with our own psychic energy, given it arms and legs, and have told ourselves that it can work for us. More than this we enshrine it in a secret place, give it a heart and a mind and the power to grant us peace and mercy.

ELIZABETH O'CONNOR

PICTURES OF
GOD'S LOVE

*This is how God showed his love among us:
He sent his one and only Son into the world
that we might live through him.*

1 JOHN 4:9 NIV

PICTURES OF GOD'S LOVE

Jesus even had love stories in his repertoire. The trio of parables recorded in Luke 15 was originally told to a group questioning Jesus for keeping company with sinners. He touched the untouchables and treated the disenfranchised with dignity. He loved those considered unacceptable and unlovable. That got him into trouble.

Jesus answered his critics with stories. He started with familiar values, the relief and joy over finding lost prized possessions. Then he told a haunting story of two brothers and a loving father, perfectly picturing God's amazing love.

As you reread these stories and ponder their lessons through the words of others, consider what role you would play in each one. Watch and listen for God's love joyfully expressed over you.

FOUND BY GOD

Now the tax collectors and "sinners" were all gathering around to hear him. But the Pharisees and the teachers of the law muttered, "This man welcomes sinners and eats with them." Then Jesus told them this parable. . . .

In all three parables which Jesus tells in response to the question of why he eats with sinners, he puts the emphasis on God's initiative. God is the shepherd who goes looking for his lost sheep. God is the woman who lights a lamp, sweeps out the house, and searches everywhere for her lost coin until she has found it. God is the father who watches and waits for his children. . . .

It might sound strange, but God wants to find me as much as, if not more than, I want to find God. . . . God is not the patriarch who stays home, doesn't move, and expects his children to come to him, apologize for their aberrant behavior, beg for forgiveness, and promise to do better. To the contrary, he leaves the house, ignoring his dignity by running toward them, pays no heed to apologies and promises of change, and brings them to the table richly prepared for them.

HENRI NOUWEN

THE GLORY OF FORGIVENESS

LUKE 15:11–13 NRSV

*Then Jesus said, "There was a man who had two sons.
The younger of them said to his father, 'Father,
give me the share of the property that will belong
to me.' So he divided his property between them.
A few days later the younger son gathered all he
had and traveled to a distant country, and there
he squandered his property in dissolute living."*

God's glory is to forgive. As the prophet Micah exclaims to Yahweh, "What god can compare with you: taking fault away, pardoning crime, not cherishing anger forever but delighting in showing mercy" (7:18). It is effortless for God to forgive. God delights in forgiveness, because his forgiveness generates new life in us. The incomparable joy of the prodigal's father in the "pearl of the parables" would have been denied if his youngest son had always been a goody-two-shoes.

Our sins are carriers of grace when they lead to repentance and authentic contrition. Like the prodigal son, we come to know an intimacy with the Father. . . . For the sins that brought us to this sacred intimacy, we are indeed grateful. They provide the opportunity for God to show mercy, which the Hebrew and Christian Scriptures testify is his greatest delight.

BRENNAN MANNING

DON'T WASTE YOUR LIFE

LUKE 15:13–14 NIV

*"Not long after that, the younger son got together all
he had, set off for a distant country and there
squandered his wealth in wild living. After he had
spent everything, there was a severe famine in that
whole country, and he began to be in need."*

This young man is known as a "prodigal" because he
wasted his father's resources. Worse, he was wasting
his life, the very worst sin against stewardship. Each one
of us has been placed on this planet by God to glorify,
honor, and serve Him with what we produce and how
we live. A wasted life is a tragedy. That was the story of
the prodigal son, until he received a new life and was
brought back to his senses.

He went back home to his father's house in repentance,
willing to give up his rights as a son and to be treated as
a hired servant. Instead, his father welcomed him home
and held a great celebration for his return—a beautiful
picture of the grace and mercy of God for prodigals of all
kinds.

R. C. SPROUL

OUR LOVING FATHER

LUKE 15:15–16 NKJV

*"Then he went and joined himself to a citizen of
that country, and he sent him into his fields
to feed swine. And he would gladly have filled
his stomach with the pods that the swine ate,
and no one gave him anything."*

There are some who, like worms wallowing in
marshes and mud, feed on foolish and useless pleasures. People are like pigs. For pigs, it is said, like mud
better than pure water. Let us not, then, be enslaved or
become like pigs. Instead, as true children of the light, let
us raise our eyes and look at light, lest the Lord discover
us to be superficial. . . . The enjoyment of many good
things is within the reach of those who love righteousness
and who pursue eternal life, especially those things which
God alludes to in Isaiah. He says, "There is an inheritance
for those who serve the Lord." Noble and desirable is this
inheritance, not gold, not silver, not clothing, that the
moths destroy, nor things of earth that robbers attack
because they are dazzled by worldly wealth. Instead, it is
the treasure of salvation which we must hurry to by
becoming lovers of the Word. . . . Consequently, our loving Father—the true Father—never stops urging, admon-
ishing, training, or loving us.

CLEMENT OF ALEXANDRIA

COME HOME

Luke 15:17–18 NIV

"When he came to his senses, he said, 'How many of my father's hired men have food to spare, and here I am starving to death! I will set out and go back to my father and say to him: "Father, I have sinned against heaven and against you."'"

I find a good many men who are living in sin, who wonder why it is that God does not answer their prayers. I will tell you why it is. God loves them too much to answer their prayers while they stay away from him. Suppose the prodigal son had written his father a letter, saying: "Father, I am in want; please send me some money." Do you suppose his father would have sent it?

If he had it would have been the worst thing he could have done for the boy. The proper thing for the prodigal to do was to go home; and just as long as his father kept him supplied with money off there in that foreign country there was no reason to expect him to come back. . . . What God wants of his "prodigal sons" is for them to come home, and when he gets them with him he will supply their wants and answer their prayers.

D. L. MOODY

WRETCHEDNESS

LUKE 15:18–19 NRSV

"I will get up and go to my father, and I will say to him, 'Father, I have sinned against heaven and before you; I am no longer worthy to be called your son; treat me like one of your hired hands.' "

Like the prodigal son, the sinful end up in the mire of the pig's slop, reduced to the greatest wretchedness, and are in a worse state than any disordered person. But when the prodigal was willing, he became suddenly young by his decision. As soon as he had said, "I will return to my Father," this one word conveyed to him all the blessings; or rather, not the word alone, but the deed which he added to the word. He did not say, "I will return," and then stay where he was.

Thus, let us also do this, no matter how far we have gotten carried away in our journey. Let us go back to our Father's house, not lingering over the length of the journey. . . . Only let us leave this strange land of sin where we have been drawn away from the Father. For our Father has a natural yearning toward us and will honor us if we are changed. He finds great pleasure in receiving back his children.

JOHN CHRYSOSTOM

WELCOMED BY GOD

LUKE 15:20 NIV

"So he got up and went to his father. But while he was still a long way off, his father saw him and was filled with compassion for him; he ran to his son, threw his arms around him and kissed him."

Most of us, most of the time, feel left out—misfits. We don't belong. Others seem to be so confident, so sure of themselves, "insiders" who know the ropes, old hands in a club from which we are excluded. One of the ways we have of responding to this is to form our own club, or join one that will have us. . . . Identity or worth is achieved by excluding all but the chosen. . . .

Jesus includes those who typically were treated as outsiders by the religious establishment of the day: women, common laborers (sheepherders), the racially different (Samaritans), the poor. He will not countenance religion as a club. As Luke tells the story all of us who have found ourselves on the outside looking in on life with no hope of gaining entrance (and who of us hasn't felt it?) now find the doors wide open, found and welcomed by God in Jesus.

EUGENE H. PETERSON

RETURN TO GOD

LUKE 15:20 NKJV
*"And he arose and came to his father. But when he
was still a great way off, his father saw him and
had compassion, and ran and fell
on his neck and kissed him."*

The grace of God is clear in this parable. The son
wasted his inheritance, hurt his father deeply, and
brought dishonor to the family name. But when he came
to his senses, the son realized that the only thing to do was
to take that long walk home and beg for forgiveness. And
not only did the father forgive him, but he provided his
son with shoes for his feet, a ring for his hand, and a joyous celebration on his behalf. "We had to celebrate this
happy day," said the father to his other son. "Your brother
was dead and has come back to life! He was lost, but now
he is found!" (Luke 15:32).

The human race is composed of prodigals. All of us
have been on the road of rebellion, seeking to find our
own way. Each individual needs to make that long walk
home! Have you returned to God? Have you renewed
that broken relationship with your Father? He is watching and waiting for your return. And he has a party
planned!

JILL BRISCOE

ACCEPTANCE

LUKE 15:20 NLT

"So he returned home to his father. And while he was still a long distance away, his father saw him coming. Filled with love and compassion, he ran to his son, embraced him, and kissed him."

The ultimate reason why we may forgive instead of condemn is because God himself does not condemn but forgives. Because he has freely chosen to put tenderness before law, we are authorized to do the same. In the imagery of the parables, God is constantly presented as the father rushing out to meet his son, the absurdly generous farmer who gives the latecomers the same wage as the day-long laborer, the judge hearing the prayer of the importunate widow. In the man Jesus the invisible God becomes visible and audible. . . . Jesus Christ taught prophetically, in the power of the Spirit, that Christian giving and forgiving should copy God's giving and forgiving. Acceptance is absolute, without inquiry into the past, without special conditions, so that the liberated sinner can live again, accept himself, forgive himself, love himself.

BRENNAN MANNING

THE FATHER'S EMBRACE

LUKE 15:21 NLT

"His son said to him, 'Father, I have sinned against both heaven and you, and I am no longer worthy of being called your son.'"

You will never be healed any other way. Do not go back to your Father's table to eat the crumbs on the floor like a dog. Think more of His redemption than that. Do not go back to your Father's house just to be safe. He wants far more for you than that. You will never heal if you only go back to your Father's home. You must go back to His heart. Closer than you've ever been.

Ah, there He is just now. Coming across the field. He is running in your direction. He doesn't even see me right now. He only has eyes for you. Forget your speeches. He wants to hug you. He wants to kiss you. Your healing will come in your very own Abba's tight and passionate embrace. Let Him hold you so close that you can hear His heart pounding from having run to you.

BETH MOORE

RESPONDING TO GOD'S LOVE

LUKE 15:27–28 NIV

"'Your brother has come . . . and your father has killed
the fattened calf because he has him back safe and
sound.' The older brother became angry and
refused to go in. So his father went out
and pleaded with him."

Unlike a fairy tale, the parable provides no happy ending. Instead it leaves us face to face with one of life's hardest spiritual choices: to trust or not to trust in God's all-forgiving love. I myself am the only one who can make that choice. In response to their complaint, "This man welcomes sinners and eats with them," Jesus confronted the Pharisees and scribes not only with the return of the prodigal son, but also with the resentful elder son. It must have come as a shock to these dutiful religious people. They finally had to face their own complaint and choose how they would respond to God's love for the sinners. . . .

The more I reflect on the elder son in me, the more I realize how deeply rooted this form of lostness really is and how hard it is to return home from there. Returning home from a lustful escapade seems so much easier than returning home from a cold anger that has rooted itself in the deepest corners of my being.

HENRI NOUWEN

PRIDE

LUKE 15:28–29 NLT
*"The older brother was angry and wouldn't go in.
His father came out and begged him, but he replied,
'All these years I've worked hard for you and never
once refused to do a single thing you told me to.
And in all that time you never gave me even
one young goat for a feast with my friends.'"*

The word sin is somehow too grand a word to apply to the reaction of the prodigal's elder brother when the sound of the hoedown reaches him out in the pasture among the cow flops, and yet in another way it is just the right word because nowhere is the deadliness of all seven of the deadly sins deadlier or more ludicrous than it is in him. Envy and pride and anger and covetousness, they are all there. Even sloth is there as he sits on his patrimony and lets it gain interest for him without lifting a hand, even lust as he slavers over the harlots whom he points out the prodigal has squandered his cash on. . . . The joke of it is that of course his father loves him even so, and has always loved him and will always love him, only the elder brother never noticed it because it was never love he was bucking for but only his due.

FREDERICK BUECHNER

UNCONDITIONAL LOVE

LUKE 15:31–32 NKJV
*"And he said to him, 'Son, you are always with me,
and all that I have is yours. It was right that we should
make merry and be glad, for your brother was dead
and is alive again, and was lost and is found.'"*

We all accept, at least with part of our minds, the parable of the Prodigal Son. We think it only right and fair that the ungrateful and spendthrift son should "fill his belly with the husks that the swine did eat." "Fair's fair," we say. But what is fair about the father running towards the returning prodigal and, before he could complete his carefully prepared speech of penitence, falling on his neck and kissing him, dressing him up in fine clothes and jewellery, and ordering food and a dance in his honour? It is just not fair, as the elder brother was quick to point out, *but it is a picture of the Love of God which is unconditional and utterly generous.*

God loves because that is His nature. . . .

When this basic certainty that God is love is grasped by our faculty and spreads into both heart and mind, it brings with it a joyous certainty.

J. B. PHILLIPS

LOVE AS GOD LOVES

1 JOHN 4:16 ESV
*So we have come to know and to believe
the love that God has for us. God is love,
and whoever abides in love abides
in God, and God abides in him.*

Father in Heaven! Thou hast loved us first, help us never to forget that Thou art love so that this sure conviction might triumph in our hearts over the seduction of the world, over the inquietude of the soul, over the anxiety for the future, over the fright of the past, over the distress of the moment. But grant also that this conviction might discipline our soul so that our heart might remain faithful and sincere in the love which we bear to all those whom Thou hast commanded us to love as we love ourselves.

PERRY D. LEFEVRE

THE GOOD SHEPHERD

MATTHEW 18:12–14 NASB

"What do you think? If any man has a hundred sheep, and one of them has gone astray, does he not leave the ninety-nine on the mountains and go and search for the one that is straying? If it turns out that he finds it, truly I say to you, he rejoices over it more than over the ninety-nine which have not gone astray. So it is not the will of your Father who is in heaven that one of these little ones perish."

Show your mercy to me, O Lord, to make my heart glad. Let me find you, for whom I long. Lo, here the man that was caught of thieves, wounded, and left for half dead, as he was going towards Jericho. You kind-hearted Samaritan, take me up. I am the sheep that is gone astray; O good Shepherd, seek me out, and bring me home to your fold again. Deal favorably with me according to your good pleasure, that I may dwell in your house all the days of my life, and praise you for ever and ever with them that are there.

ST. JEROME

THE LORD IS MY SHEPHERD

MATTHEW 18:12–13 NLT

"If a shepherd has one hundred sheep, and one wanders away and is lost, what will he do? Won't he leave the ninety-nine others and go out into the hills to search for the lost one? And if he finds it, he will surely rejoice over it more than over the ninety-nine that didn't wander away!"

I like to think of Christ as a shepherd. The duty of a shepherd is to take care of his sheep. When a bear attacked David's flock, he seized his spear and slew the intruder, and your Shepherd will take as much care of you.

Oh, what joy in the news to those who can say, "The Lord is my shepherd" (Psalm 23:1). Think of the shepherd carefully counting his sheep at the close of the day; one is missing; what does he do? Is he content with his ninety and nine, leaving the missing? No, he safely houses the others and then goes in search of the missing one. Can you not see him hunting for the lost one, going over mountains and rocks and crossing brooks? And what joy there is when the wanderer is found. Oh, what a shepherd is that!

D. L. MOODY

THERE IS HOPE

LUKE 15:5 NASB

*"When he has found it, he lays it
on his shoulders, rejoicing."*

These parables are Christ's defense of His ministry, explaining why He fellowshipped with sinners and even ate with them.

He saw what they were. They were sheep that had gone astray and needed a shepherd to bring them home. They were back into circulation again. They were disobedient sons who were wasting their inheritance and needed to come home to the Father.

He saw how they got that way. Sheep are foolish animals and naturally go astray, but the spiritual shepherds in Israel had not faithfully ministered to them (Jeremiah 23; Ezekiel 34). The woman lost the coin because of carelessness, and the son was lost because of his willfulness. . . .

He saw what they could be. Jesus always saw the potential in people. The sheep could be brought back to the flock and bring joy to the shepherd; the coin could be found; and the son could return home and lovingly serve his father. There is hope for every sinner because Jesus welcomes everyone.

WARREN W. WIERSBE

GOD REACHED DOWN

MATTHEW 18:14 NKJV

"Even so it is not the will of your Father who is in heaven that one of these little ones should perish."

I found myself after that [suicide] attempt lying in a hospital bed, having expelled all the poison that I had taken but unsure if I would recover. There on that bed, with a dehydrated body, the Scriptures were read to me. The flooding of my heart with the news that Jesus Christ could come into my life and that I could know God personally defies the depths to which the truth overwhelmed me. In that moment with a simple prayer of trust, the change from a desperate heart to one that found the fullness of meaning became a reality for me.

God reached down to a teenager in a hospital bed in the city of New Delhi, a mega-city of teeming millions. Imagine! God cared enough to hear my cry. How incredible, that He has a personal interest in the struggles of our lives. . . . That was the point of the parable Jesus told about the shepherd who left the ninety-nine sheep in the fold and went looking for the one.

RAVI ZACHARIAS

KNOWING THE SHEPHERD

MATTHEW 18:14 ESV

*"So it is not the will of my Father who is in heaven
that one of these little ones should perish."*

There's a true story I love about a house party in one of
the big English country houses. Often after dinner at
these parties people give recitations, sing, and use whatever
talent they have to entertain the company. One year a
famous actor was among the guests. . . . When it came his
turn to perform, he recited the Twenty-third Psalm. . . .
His rendition was magnificent, and there was much
applause. At the end of the evening someone noticed a
little old great aunt dozing in the corner. She . . . was
urged to get up and recite something. . . . In her quavery
old voice she started, *The Lord is my shepherd* . . . When
she had finished there were tears in many eyes. Later one
of the guests approached the famous actor. "You recited
that psalm absolutely superbly. It was incomparable. So
why were we so moved by that funny, little old lady?"

He replied, "I know the psalm. She knows the shepherd."

MADELEINE L'ENGLE

CHRIST'S EXAMPLE

LUKE 15:10 NASB
*"In the same way, I tell you, there is joy
in the presence of the angels of God
over one sinner who repents."*

Christ is both the shepherd and the woman; for he has lighted the lamp, that is, the Gospel, and he goes about in the desert, that is, the world. He sweeps the house, and seeks the lost sheep and lost piece of silver, when he comes with his Word and proclaims to us, first our sins, and then his grace and mercy. . . .

Learn from this, then, that our neighbor is to be sought as a lost sheep, that his shame is to be covered with our honor, that our piety is to be a cover for his sins. . . . Therefore, ye men, whenever ye come together, do not backbite your neighbors. Make not one face at one person and another at someone else. Do not cut off one man's foot and another man's hand; make no such traffic of living flesh. Likewise, ye women, when you come together, conceal the shame of others, and do not cause wounds which you cannot heal.

MARTIN LUTHER

THE INSPIRING POWER OF LOVE

1 THESSALONIANS 1:3 ESV
*. . . remembering before our God and Father your work
of faith and labor of love and steadfastness
of hope in our Lord Jesus Christ.*

What can turn the statutes into songs, take the sting out of the commandments, make the will of God a delight? When it is all transfigured by the glory of love. Love inspires obedience to law, and makes it easy. . . . When we are brought into a personal relation to God and enter into fellowship with Him, we realize that even in the making of our own moral life, in the creating of our own character, we are fellow-workers with God. We desire the same end as He does, and it is the best end.

The love of Christ is the great instrument of sanctification; for it breeds in us a passion to do God's will and keep His commandments. 'Ye are complete in Him,' says St. Paul. He fills out our incompleteness, and for the first time we feel that we are truly ourselves. . . . When our heart is enlarged we can run in the way of God's commandments. Life breaks out into music and light.

HUGH BLACK

THE LORD OF LOVE

JOHN 13:13 NIV
"You call me 'Teacher' and 'Lord,' and rightly so,
for that is what I am."

Napoleon, conversing in exile one day at St. Helena, as his custom was, about the great men of antiquity and comparing himself with them, said: "Alexander, Caesar, Charlemagne, and myself founded great empires, but upon what did the creations of our genius depend? Upon force. Jesus alone founded His kingdom upon love, and to this day millions would die for Him." True indeed! Upon love Jesus established His monarchy. His empire is a monarchy of love, not a democracy, not a republic, but an absolute monarchy based upon supreme loyalty to Him, and governed throughout by love. Broad and extended, yet never exceeding the limits of love. This is Christ's kingdom, and this is the manner of His government; a kingdom worthy of a human, and worthy, also, in every way of a divine Christ.

GEORGE LIVINGSTONE ROBINSON

KNOWING GOD'S LOVE

---

1 JOHN 4:8 NIV
Whoever does not love does not know God,
because God is love.

T he statement "God *is* love" means that his love finds
expression in everything that he says and does. The
knowledge that this is true for each of us personally is our
supreme comfort as Christians. As believers, we find in
the Cross of Christ assurance that we, as individuals, are
beloved of God. Each of us can say with truth, "The Son
of God . . . loved me and gave himself for me" (Galatians
2:20). Knowing this, he is able to apply to himself the
promise that all things work together for good to those
who love God and are called according to his purpose
(Romans 8:28). Not just *some* things, note, but *all* things!

. . . Even when he cannot see the why and wherefore
of God's dealings, he knows that there is love in and
behind them and so he can rejoice always; even when,
humanly speaking, things are going wrong, he knows that
the true story of his life, when known, will prove to be
"mercy from first to last"—and he is content.

J. I. PACKER

HIS PARABLES   271

PERSEVERE

LUKE 15:8 NIV

*"Or suppose a woman has ten silver coins and
loses one. Does she not light a lamp,
sweep the house and search carefully
until she finds it?"*

This woman *sought for her piece of silver continuously*—
"till she found it." May you and I, as parts of the
church of God, look after wandering souls till we find
them. We say they discourage us. No doubt that piece of
silver did discourage the woman who sought it. We com-
plain that men do not appear inclined to religion. Did the
piece of money lend the housewife any help? Was it any
assistance to her? She did the seeking, she did it all. And
the Holy Ghost through you, my brother, seeks the salvation of the sinner, not expecting the sinner to help him,
for the sinner is averse to being found. What, were you
repulsed the other day by one whose spiritual good you
longed for? Go again! . . . A harsh reception is sometimes
only an intimation that the heart recognises the power of
the truth, though it does not desire at present to yield to
it. Persevere, brother, till you find the soul you seek.

C. H. SPURGEON

THERE'S HOPE

LUKE 15:8 NASB

*"Or what woman, if she has ten silver coins and
loses one coin, does not light a lamp
and sweep the house and search carefully
until she finds it?"*

Hope is not refusing to face the truth. Hope is having a confidence in God to see you through each difficult trial. Jesus was always the epitome of truth, but He never failed to bring hope to others. When He met the woman taken in adultery, He inspired her to hope again. When he met the thief on the cross, Jesus made sure that man left this life with hope. He told the story about the lost coin that was found, and the lost son who came home, and the lost sheep that was found. Over and over again, what Jesus said in His messages was, "There's hope!" Though He was mocked, disbelieved, and crucified, He never doubted the glory that was yet to be, and He endured the cross for the joy that was set before Him. He had hope.

Love hangs on with tenacity when other hands let go in despair. To hope when faith has been disappointed is a greater thing than to have believed the sure thing. Love hopes all things.

DAVID JEREMIAH

FOLLOWING CHRIST'S EXAMPLE

LUKE 15:9–10 NRSV

*"When she has found it, she calls together her friends
and neighbors, saying, 'Rejoice with me, for I have
found the coin that I had lost.' Just so, I tell you,
there is joy in the presence of the angels
of God over one sinner who repents."*

As the house of the woman was filled with happiness
and laughter because that which was lost had been
found, so heaven rejoices when a sinner repents and turns
to God in faith. . . .

Jesus showed God's love to the "sinners" of his day. He
taught the publicans and moral outcasts, he entered their
homes, he ate and drank with them, and he was given the
name "friend of sinners" (Matthew 11:19). Because of
this, the Pharisees considered even Jesus to be a sinner.

The two parables of the sheep and the coin have a definite evangelistic thrust. The church, known as the body
of Christ, is called to extend love and concern to the
men, women, and children who are spiritually lost in this
world. . . . The fervor Jesus displayed in associating with
the so-called "sinners" of his day must glow in every
member of the church, radiating the warmth of evangelistic zeal, and rejoicing with "the angels of God over one
sinner who repents."

SIMON KISTEMAKER

LIVING ETERNAL LIFE

EPHESIANS 2:4–6 ESV
*But God, being rich in mercy, because of the great love
with which he loved us, even when we were dead in
our trespasses, made us alive together with Christ—
by grace you have been saved—and raised
us up with him and seated us with him
in the heavenly places in Christ Jesus.*

We think of Eternal Life, if we think of it at all, as what happens when life ends. We would do better to think of it as what happens when life begins.

St. Paul uses the phrase Eternal Life to describe the end and goal of the process of salvation. Elsewhere he writes the same thing in a remarkable sentence in which he says that the whole purpose of God's slogging around through the muck of history and of our own individual histories is somehow to prod us, jolly us, worry us, cajole us, and if need be, bludgeon us into reaching "mature manhood . . . the measure of the stature of the fullness of Christ" (Ephesians 4:13).

In other words, to live Eternal Life in the full and final sense is to be with God as Christ is with him, and with each other as Christ is with us.

FREDERICK BUECHNER

HUMILITY

ROMANS 5:5 KJV
*And hope maketh not ashamed;
because the love of God is shed abroad
in our hearts by the Holy Ghost
which is given unto us.*

When the spirit of love is shed abroad in the heart, when the divine nature comes to a full birth, when Christ the meek and lowly Lamb of God is truly formed within, there is given the power of a perfect love that forgets itself and finds its blessedness in blessing others, in bearing with them and honoring them, however weak they may be. When this love enters, God enters. When God has entered in His power, and reveals Himself as All, the person becomes nothing. When a person becomes nothing before God, that person cannot be anything but humble toward others.

The presence of God becomes not a thing of times and seasons, but the covering under which the soul always dwells. Its deep humility before God then becomes the holy place of His presence from which all its words and works proceed.

ANDREW MURRAY

THE LOVE OF CHRIST

JOHN 3:16 ESV
*"For God so loved the world, that he gave
his only Son, that whoever believes in him
should not perish but have eternal life."*

The mercy of heaven is big enough to take in all our sinful race. The blood of Christ is rich enough to cover the guilt of every child of Adam. The gospel is broad enough to take in whosoever will. The life of Jesus Christ is full enough to save and sanctify and keep all the myriads of our race, if they will but accept it. The heaven that He has provided is vast enough for all earth's lost generations. And the divine plan is grand enough to take in every kindred and tribe and tongue, all earth's countless inhabitants. There may be limitations in the receiving of God's grace on our part through the ignorance, willfulness or indifference of sinful men, but there is no limitation to the sufficiency of Christ's redemption and the universal and all-embracing fullness of the gospel of salvation.

A. B. SIMPSON

PARABLES OF MERCY

MATTHEW 13:10 NLT
His disciples came and asked him,
"Why do you always tell stories
when you talk to the people?"

To move through the language and imagery of Jesus' parables offers some fascinating insights into his sensibilities. Noah Webster defines an iconoclast as "one who makes attacks on cherished beliefs and institutions, one who destroys or opposes the veneration of religious images." Jesus, the master storyteller, was clearly an iconoclast. His parables expressed in words what his actions demonstrated. He shattered idols and blew away preconceived ideas of who God is and what men and women are meant to be.

The parables of divine mercy—especially those about a lost coin, a lost sheep, and a lost son—are rooted in Jesus' own experience of his Father. In these parables and others, Jesus speaks wholly and entirely in the light of this reality. The stories were intended, not only to defend his own notorious conduct with sinners, but to startle his critics and stand them on their heads by cracking through their conventional way of thinking about God.

BRENNAN MANNING

PICTURES OF
THANKFULNESS

—

Give thanks in all circumstances,
for this is God's will for you
in Christ Jesus.

1 THESSALONIANS 5:18 NIV

PICTURES OF THANKFULNESS

Gratitude extends well beyond words. Expressions like "thank you" can be empty of meaning if not backed up with action. The depth of our gratitude can be measured by what we do when the positions are reversed. The generosity of another that leads to gratefulness on our part gives us the opportunity to pass on generosity to someone else. Jesus taught that those who have been forgiven much and those who are truly thankful give others reasons to be thankful. Those who are not generous are seldom thankful.

The readings in this section will help you reflect on the ways you express gratitude. They will also lead you to consider how you respond to God's generosity toward you. You may find yourself giving thanks in new ways.

THE KING'S HEART OF FORGIVENESS

LUKE 7:41–43 NKJV

"There was a certain creditor who had two debtors.
One owed five hundred denarii, and the other fifty.
And when they had nothing with which to repay,
he freely forgave them both. Tell Me, therefore,
which of them will love him more?" Simon answered
and said, "I suppose the one whom he forgave more."
And He said to him, "You have rightly judged."

At the heart of the kingdom of heaven is the King's heart of forgiveness. . . . Our sin is rebellion against God: the willful desire to run our own lives, to shape our own destiny, to live by our own strength and grit. How can we repay the debt we owe for the ravage we make of our lives? We can't. . . . And lo! The King responds to our plea. He sends His only Son, Jesus, to save His people from their sins.

LLOYD JOHN OGILVIE

CHEAP FORGIVENESS

LUKE 7:41–43 NLT
*Then Jesus told him this story: "A man loaned
money to two people—five hundred pieces
of silver to one and fifty pieces to the other.
But neither of them could repay him,
so he kindly forgave them both, canceling their debts.
Who do you suppose loved him more after that?"
Simon answered, "I suppose the one
for whom he canceled the larger debt."
"That's right," Jesus said.*

Forgiving others "from your heart" is a burred hook. We can't slip off by saying we will forgive but not forget. Or that we will forgive the person, but not the deed. Cheap forgiveness! Verbalism without a vital, reconciled relationship. All such measures are ways of trying to evade the responsibility of reproducing in our own lives the awesome completeness of God's forgiveness of us. . . . What has happened since we were born again and received new life? Has it made any difference? Have we forgiven as we've been forgiven? Has our attitude to people around us been consistent with God's acceptance of us?

LLOYD JOHN OGILVIE

FORGIVENESS CAUSES LOVE

LUKE 7:42 NIV
*"Neither of them had the money to pay
him back, so he canceled the debts of both.
Now which of them will love him more?"*

Love is not the cause of forgiveness. Forgiveness causes
love. The more we are forgiven, the more we love.

If we fill our thoughts with sin and damnation and the
wrath of God that condemns us before we are born, we
cannot love God. We will hate him as a tyrant and run
away from him. But when the gospel of Christ demonstrates how God loves us first, forgives us, and has mercy
on us, then we love again. . . .

We also say, "If you don't love my dog, you don't love
me." Maybe the dog does not deserve it. Perhaps he has
even brought you displeasure. Yet if you love me, you will
refrain from revenging yourself against my dog. In the first
letter of John we read, "We love each other as a result of
his loving us first. If someone says, 'I love God,' but hates
a Christian brother or sister, that person is a liar" (1 John
4:19–20). I am commanded to love. If I do not love this
commandment, I do not love God.

WILLIAM TYNDALE

THE EVER-WATCHING GOD

LUKE 7:43 NRSV
Simon answered, "I suppose the one for
whom he canceled the greater debt." And Jesus
said to him, "You have judged rightly."

Begin with thanking Him for some little thing, and then go on, day by day, adding to your subjects of praise; thus you will find their numbers grow wonderfully; and, in the same proportion, will your subjects of murmuring and complaining diminish, until you see in everything some cause for thanksgiving. If you cannot begin with anything positive, begin with something negative. If your whole lot seems only filled with causes for discontent, at any rate there is some trial that has *not* been appointed you; and you may thank God for its being withheld from you. It is certain that the more you try to praise, the more you will see how your path and your lying down are beset with mercies, and that the God of love is ever watching to do you good.

PRISCILLA MAURICE

SPEECHLESS

PSALM 92:1 NIV
It is good to praise the LORD
and make music to your name, O Most High.

O God, you are the greatest and the best,
   The strongest, the most merciful and just,
Absolutely concealed and absolutely present,
Beautiful, mysterious,
Never changing, but changing everything,
Never new, yet never old,
Always in action, yet always at rest,
Attracting all things to yourself but needing none,
Preserving and fulfilling and sheltering,
Conceiving and nourishing and ripening,
Continually seeking but lacking nothing,
You love without the confusion of emotion,
You are jealous, but without fear.
You owe us nothing, and yet you give to us as though
     you were indebted to us.
You forgive what is due you and yet lose nothing
     yourself.

After all this, what have I said? What can anyone say
     when speaking of God?

AUGUSTINE

GIVING THANKS

COLOSSIANS 3:15 ESV
And let the peace of Christ rule in your hearts,
to which indeed you were called in one body.
And be thankful.

In the Christian community thankfulness is just what it is anywhere else in the Christian life. Only he who gives thanks for little things receives the big things. We prevent God from giving us the great spiritual gifts He has in store for us, because we do not give thanks for daily gifts. We think we dare not be satisfied with the small measure of spiritual knowledge, experience, and love that has been given to us, and that we must constantly be looking forward eagerly for the highest good. Then we deplore the fact that we lack the deep certainty, the strong faith, and the rich experience that God has given to others, and we consider this lament to be pious. We pray for the big things and forget to give thanks for the ordinary, small (and yet really not small) gifts. How can God entrust great things to one who will not thankfully receive from Him the little things?

DIETRICH BONHOEFFER

COMFORT IN CHRIST

LUKE 23:34 NIV

*Jesus said, "Father, forgive them, for they
do not know what they are doing." And they
divided up his clothes by casting lots.*

We must remember the value of right belief. It is profitable for me to know that Christ bore my diseases and submitted Himself to my lusts for my sake. He became sin and a curse for me—for everyone, that is. He was humbled and became a servant for me. . . . What a glorious remedy—to have comfort in Christ! For He bore these things with enormous patience for our sakes—so we definitely can't bear them just for the glory of His name with common patience! Who wouldn't learn to forgive their enemies when they see that, even on the cross, Christ prayed for those who persecuted Him? Don't you see that the weaknesses of Christ's are your strength? So why do you ask Him about remedies for us? His tears wash us and His weeping cleanses us. . . . But if you begin to doubt, you will despair. For the greater the insult, the greater gratitude is due.

AMBROSE

THE WEALTH OF AGE

1 THESSALONIANS 5:18 NLT
*No matter what happens, always be thankful,
for this is God's will for you who
belong to Christ Jesus.*

There is a wealth in age gained only by the living of it. Only those who have routinely left and lost parts of life and gone on living can show the rest of the world that what the world calls unsurvivable—humiliation, scarcity, failure, loss—can, indeed, be survived. And often for the best.

. . . Age is a mirror of the knowledge of God. Age teaches that time is precious, that companionship is better than wealth, that sitting can be as much a spiritual discipline as running marathons, that thinking is superior to doing, that learning is eternal, that things go to dust, that adult toys wear thin with time, that only what is within us—good music, fine reading, great art, thoughtful conversation, faith, and God—remains. When our mountain climbing days are over, the elderly know, these are the things that will chart the setting of our suns and walk us to our graves. All the doings will wash away; all the being will emerge.

JOAN D. CHITTISTER

GIVING THANKS

LUKE 17:17–19 NIV
Jesus asked, "Were not all ten cleansed?
Where are the other nine? Was no one found
to return and give praise to God except
this foreigner?" Then he said to him,
"Rise and go; your faith has made you well."

One of the most instructive passages on the subject of thankfulness is Luke 17:11–19, the account of the healing of the ten lepers. . . .

As these men went to show themselves to the priest and thus be restored to their families and friends, only one of them, realizing what had happened, turned back to give thanks to Jesus. Ten men were healed, but only one gave thanks. How prone we are to be like the other nine. We are anxious to receive but too careless to give thanks. We pray for God's intervention in our lives, then congratulate ourselves rather than God for the results. When one of the American lunar missions was in serious trouble some years ago, the American people were asked to pray for the safe return of the astronauts. When they were safely back on earth, credit was given to the technological achievements and skill of the American space industry. No thanks or credit was publicly given to God. This is not unusual. It is the natural tendency of mankind.

JERRY BRIDGES

FORGIVENESS AND LOVE

LUKE 7:43 ESV
Simon answered, "The one, I suppose,
for whom he cancelled the larger debt."
And he said to him, "You have judged rightly."

Then Jesus asked Simon to summarize which debtor loved the moneylender most. The answer was obvious, but Simon's words "I suppose" revealed his reluctance to acknowledge it. After Simon pinpointed the one with the bigger debt canceled, Christ said, "You have judged correctly" (v. 43). . . .

Christ then brought the parable to life. He compared their responses to Him. All three times Christ's description of the Pharisee's actions began with the unsettling words, "You did not." How poignant. You see, one of the surest signs of an ancient or modern-day "Pharisee" is a life characterized far more by what he or she does not do than what he or she does. . . .

He packs the punch into the living parable in verse 47: "Therefore, I tell you, her many sins have been forgiven—for she loved much. But he who has been forgiven little loves little." Not because that's the way it has to be, but because that's the reality of our human tendency.

BETH MOORE AND DALE McCLESKEY

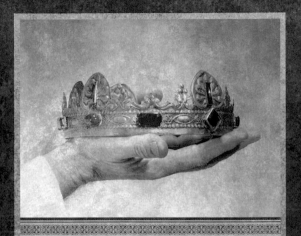

PICTURES OF
GOD'S RULE

---

*The Root of Jesse will spring up,
one who will arise to rule over the nations;
the Gentiles will hope in him.*
ROMANS 15:12 NIV

PICTURES OF GOD'S RULE

How does the holy, righteous, and loving God deal with unholy, unrighteous, and unloving people? The answers are found in some of Jesus' sharpest-edged stories. At least five parables present case studies of someone in authority dealing with more-or-less obedient servants. The pictures are not pretty. And yet, they are hopeful. Those who offer God an honest "no" fare better than those who put God off with excuses and deceit. Initial denial can often give way to acceptance. Unfortunately, superficial belief often leads to hardened rejection.

Don't miss the demands of God's holiness at the center of the stories. They require a response from you. The readings in this section will give you glimpses of the awesome character of God, and they will invite you to examine your own life in the light of all that God has done for you.

PATIENCE

MATTHEW 18:23–26 NRSV
*"For this reason the kingdom of heaven may be
compared to a king who wished to settle accounts
with his slaves. When he began the reckoning, one who
owed him ten thousand talents was brought to him;
and, as he could not pay, his lord ordered him to be
sold, together with his wife and children and all his
possessions, and payment to be made. So the slave
fell on his knees before him, saying, 'Have patience
with me, and I will pay you everything.'"*

The word patience makes a surprise appearance here.
The debtor does not plead for mercy or forgiveness;
he pleads for patience. Equally curious is this singular
appearance of the word. Jesus uses it twice in this story
and never again. It appears nowhere else in the Gospels.
Perhaps the scarce usage is the first-century equivalent of
a highlighter. Jesus reserves the word for one occasion to
make one point. Patience is more than a virtue for long
lines and slow waiters. Patience is the red carpet upon
which God's grace approaches us.

MAX LUCADO

THE MEASURE OF FORGIVENESS

MATTHEW 18:28-30 NLT

*"But when the man left the king, he went to
a fellow servant who owed him a few thousand
dollars. He grabbed him by the throat and demanded
instant payment. His fellow servant fell down before
him and begged for a little more time. 'Be patient
and I will pay it,' he pleaded. But his creditor
wouldn't wait. He had the man arrested and
jailed until the debt could be paid in full."*

The reason why forgiveness must be unlimited is
explained in a vivid parable. The unimaginable size
of the original debt . . . is picked up in the emphatic *all
that debt* of v. 32. If that is the measure of the forgiveness
the disciple has received, any limitation on the forgiveness
he shows to his brother is unthinkable. The fact that the
second servant's debt is one six-hundred-thousandth of
the first emphasizes the ludicrous impropriety of the forgiven sinner's standing on his own 'rights'. . . .

If the church is the community of the forgiven, then all
its relationships will be marked by a forgiveness which is
not a mere form of words, but an essential characteristic;
from your heart excludes all casuistry and legalism.

R. T. FRANCE

UNMERITED GIFTS

MATTHEW 18:32–35 ESV

"Then his master summoned him and said to him,
'You wicked servant! I forgave you all that debt
because you pleaded with me. And should not you
have had mercy on your fellow servant, as I had mercy
on you?' And in anger his master delivered him to the
jailers, until he should pay all his debt. So also my
heavenly Father will do to every one of you, if you
do not forgive your brother from your heart."

Here we may find the explanation for why the great saints spoke frequently about their sinfulness. Motivated not by masochism, false modesty, or low self-esteem, but by gratitude, they grew into an ever-deepening awareness that their passion for Christ, their heroic life of prayer, and their unstinting generosity in ministry were all unmerited gifts. They also grew to realize how often they forgot their giftedness. The parable of the merciless debtor clearly states that we sin against God if we fail to forgive the petty grievances of our neighbor. But the truth is that we sin every day, whenever we fail to be grateful to God for his manifold gifts.

BRENNAN MANNING

SUBMITTING TO GOD

MATTHEW 21:28–31 NLT

*"But what do you think about this? A man with
two sons told the older boy, 'Son, go out and work
in the vineyard today.' The son answered, 'No, I won't
go,' but later he changed his mind and went anyway.
Then the father told the other son, 'You go,' and
he said, 'Yes, sir, I will.' But he didn't go. Which of
the two was obeying his father?" They replied, "The
first, of course." Then Jesus explained his meaning:
"I assure you, corrupt tax collectors and prostitutes
will get into the Kingdom of God before you do."*

This conclusion shows what is the object of the parable . . . Christ tells them that it is quite as if *a son*
were, in words, to promise obedience to *his father,* but
afterwards to deceive him. So far as regards *the publicans
and the harlots,* he does not excuse their vices, but compares their dissolute life to the obstinacy of a rebellious
and debauched *son,* who at first throws off his father's
authority; but shows that they are greatly preferable to the
scribes and Pharisees in this respect, that they do not continue to the end in their vices, but, on the contrary, submit gently and obediently to the yoke which they had
fiercely rejected.

JOHN CALVIN

THE MERCY OF GOD

LUKE 13:7–9 NIV

" . . . 'For three years now I've been coming to look
for fruit on this fig tree and haven't found any.
Cut it down! Why should it use up the soil?'
'Sir,' the man replied, 'leave it alone for one more
year, and I'll dig around it and fertilize it. If it
bears fruit next year, fine! If not, then cut it down.'"

Now comes a parable that brings out two things: the need for repentance and God's slowness to punish. . . .

Jesus sets the scene with a fig tree in a vineyard (and thus in fertile soil). The owner has been looking for fruit for three years, which seems to indicate a well-established tree. A failure to bear for three years sounds ominous. It was unlikely that such a tree would bear again. . . .

The vinedresser counsels patience. Perhaps treatment of the soil and the application of manure for a further year will bring results. It will give the tree one last chance to produce. But the vinedresser recognizes facts. If it still does not bear that is the end of the matter. . . . The fact that evil is not punished here and now does not mean that God approves of what sinners are doing; it means that to the end God is merciful.

LEON MORRIS

THE NEED FOR FRUIT

LUKE 13:7–9 NLT

"Finally, he said to his gardener, 'I've waited three years, and there hasn't been a single fig! Cut it down. It's taking up space we can use for something else.' The gardener answered, 'Give it one more chance. Leave it another year, and I'll give it special attention and plenty of fertilizer. If we get figs next year, fine. If not, you can cut it down.'"

Jesus talked a lot about fruitfulness throughout His ministry. False prophets can be identified by their fruits; every good tree bears good fruit, but the rotten tree bears bad fruit. . . . Jesus' judgment on Israel was that although they were the tree of God, they had produced only the leaves of religion—the external appearances—but not the fruit of righteousness. . . . The message here is timeless. It speaks to the Church in every age. The danger of leaves without fruit is ever present.

LLOYD JOHN OGILVIE

GOD'S GENEROSITY

PSALM 145:9 NASB
*The LORD is good to all,
And His mercies are over all His works.*

Generosity means a disposition to give to others in a way which has no mercenary motive and is not limited by what the recipients deserve, but consistently goes beyond it. Generosity expresses the simple wish that others should have what they need to make them happy. Generosity is, so to speak, the focal point of God's moral perfection; it is the quality which determines how all God's other excellences are to be displayed.

. . . There is God's generosity in bestowing natural blessings: every meal, every pleasure, every possession, every bit of sun, every night's sleep, every moment of safety, everything else that sustains and enriches life (Psalm 145). But the mercies of God on the natural level, however abundant, are overshadowed by the greater mercies of spiritual redemption: God's mighty acts in saving Israel from Egypt; his willingness to forbear and forgive when his servants fall into sin; his readiness to teach men his way; his mercy in grafting "wild" Gentiles into his olive tree (Psalm 106; 86:5; 119:68; Romans 11:22).

J. I. PACKER

VITAL LINKS

MATTHEW 22:1–3 ESV

*And again Jesus spoke to them in parables, saying,
"The kingdom of heaven may be compared to a king
who gave a wedding feast for his son, and sent his
servants to call those who were invited to
the wedding feast, but they would not come."*

We must realize, therefore, that when God sends us to evangelize, He sends us to act as vital links in the chain of His purpose for the salvation of His elect. The fact that He has such a purpose, and that it is (so we believe) a sovereign purpose that cannot be thwarted, does not imply that, after all, our evangelizing is not needed for its fulfillment. In our Lord's parable, the way in which the wedding was furnished with guests was through the action of the king's servants, who went out as they were bidden into the highways and invited in all whom they found there. Hearing the invitation, the passersby came. It is in the same way, and through similar action by the servants of God, that the elect come into the salvation that the Redeemer has won for them.

J. I. PACKER

THE TIME IS NOW

MATTHEW 22:5–7 NIV

*"But they paid no attention and went off—one
to his field, another to his business. The rest seized
his servants, mistreated them and killed them. The
king was enraged. He sent his army and destroyed
those murderers and burned their city."*

The kingdom has come! If those invited exclude
themselves from the kingdom, then others will take
(and are taking) their place. The excuses offered appear
quite valid, excuses for rejecting Christ and his kingdom
frequently do, but the result is the same—exclusion from
the kingdom! . . . The point of the parable for Jesus, however, lies not so much with the demand of the kingdom,
for most people would have accepted the view that God's
demand is absolute. What Jesus is interacting with here is
the concept that the kingdom of God is future—"Blessed
is he who *shall* eat bread in the kingdom of God." The
kingdom has already come, however. The table is already
prepared and all is now ready. The invitation has gone
forth. . . . Now is the time of salvation! If the religious
elite of Israel will not enter the kingdom now, it will be
too late. They will never taste the banquet, and others will
take their place!

ROBERT H. STEIN

STOP STUFFING YOURSELF

MATTHEW 22:5, 7 NLT

"But the guests he had invited ignored them and went about their business, one to his farm, another to his store. . . . Then the king became furious. He sent out his army to destroy the murderers and burn their city."

If you get up Thanksgiving morning and eat a loaf of white bread for breakfast, Thanksgiving dinner will not sound attractive when someone calls you with an invitation at mid-morning. Some preferred land to God. Some preferred cows to God. And some preferred wives to God. And none of them will be at the eternal banquet, Jesus says.

To make this clear Jesus tells two more parables in Luke 14:25–33. We've seen that the invitation goes out indiscriminately to all. Then in verse 25 multitudes start to respond. "Now great multitudes accompanied him." But Jesus clarifies a few things before they get very far with their excitement. He says in effect, "To enjoy the table of God you must stop stuffing yourself with the local cuisine."

. . . The banquet hall is big! The food is delicious! The invitation to come is sent to all! But the entrance requirement is that you are more hungry for what God serves than for what the world serves.

JOHN PIPER

There Is No Merit

Matthew 22:8–10 NIV

*"Then he said to his servants, 'The wedding banquet
is ready, but those I invited did not deserve to come.
Go to the street corners and invite to the banquet
anyone you find.' So the servants went out into
the streets and gathered all the people they could find,
both good and bad, and the wedding hall
was filled with guests."*

Could this be the coming of the Kingdom of God,
when all the moral safeguards laboriously built up
by the teachers of the Law were cast aside, and the law-
less were welcomed into fellowship? To those who raise
such objections Jesus appealed in parables with an ironi-
cal point. If invited guests do not come to a feast, something must be done to fill the vacant seats. And if a son
who made fair promises fails to fulfill them, credit is surely
due to the other son who atones for his first rudeness by
a tardy obedience. . . . But, in fact, there is no such thing
as merit in the sight of God. If He bestows His gifts upon
men who have done nothing to deserve them, He is like
a magnificently generous employer who pays a full day's
wage for an hour's work. The Kingdom of God is like
that.

C. H. Dodd

SPEECHLESS

MATTHEW 22:11–12 ESV

*"But when the king came in to look at the guests,
he saw there a man who had no wedding garment.
And he said to him, 'Friend, how did you get in here
without a wedding garment?' And he was speechless."*

He who was the unworthy guest is now the criminal at the feast. The king has now become a judge to him; the question has been personally put to him, and he is *speechless*. Why is he silent? Surely it was because he was convicted of open, undeniable disloyalty. No evidence was required; he had come there on set purpose with malice aforethought to display his disloyalty, and had done so in the presence of the King. I do not think he represents at all a person who enters the church through ignorance, with a sincere but ignorant intention. . . . He is a man willing to be saved by grace, and professing to be so, but refusing to acknowledge his duty to God and his obligations to the Son. He was speechless; he could not have chosen a worse place, nor a more impertinent method of ventilating his disloyalty than that which he selected; there was nothing he could say in self-defense.

C. H. SPURGEON

BE PREPARED

MATTHEW 22:13 ESV

"Then the king said to the attendants, 'Bind him hand and foot and cast him into the outer darkness. In that place there will be weeping and gnashing of teeth.'"

There is extraordinary power in storytelling that stirs the imagination and makes an indelible impression on the mind. Jesus employs a set of stories, known as the 'crisis' parables to issue a warning, a summons to repentance, because of the lateness of the hour. Jesus says, "A tidal wave is approaching and you are lollygagging on the patio having a party." Or as Joachim Jeremias puts it, "You are feasting and dancing—on the volcano which may erupt at any moment." The impending crisis precludes procrastination. "Stay awake, because you do not know when the master of the house is coming, evening, midnight, cockcrow, dawn; if he comes unexpectedly, he must not find you asleep. . . .'"

In the parable of the wedding feast, the guest without a wedding garment is forcibly seized by the bouncers and heaved out the door. "The festal garment is repentance. Put it on today before your death, the day before the Deluge breaks, put it on today! The demand of the crisis is conversion."

BRENNAN MANNING

THE REWARDS OF SURRENDER

PSALM 119:165 NCV
Those who love your teachings will find true peace,
and nothing will defeat them.

What you need to do, is to put your will over completely into the hands of your Lord, surrendering to Him the entire control of it. Say, "Yes, Lord, YES!" to everything, and trust Him so to work in you to will, as to bring your whole wishes and affections into conformity with His own sweet, and lovable, and most lovely will. It is wonderful what miracles God works in wills that are utterly surrendered to Him. He turns hard things into easy, and bitter things into sweet. It is not that He puts easy things in the place of the hard, but He actually changes the hard thing into an easy one.

HANNAH WHITALL SMITH

PICTURES OF
SPIRITUAL
LIVING

"I am the vine; you are the branches.
If a man remains in me and I in him,
he will bear much fruit;
apart from me you can do nothing."
JOHN 15:5 NIV

PICTURES OF SPIRITUAL LIVING

Parables represent a way of thinking and speaking. Jesus' language was filled with word pictures. He captured vivid ideas with simple expressions like "living water" and "born again." Our familiarity with those terms often results in a lack of attentiveness. When Jesus first spoke them, they provoked quite a response.

Jesus retrieved some of His words from long forgotten or neglected passages of Scripture. Others He chose from life, creating unexpected connections between familiar words and unfamiliar ideas. His use of terms like "door" and "branch" took the concept of personification to a whole new level. He took the common things of life and made them into the uncommon things of spiritual life.

As you read the following reflections on Jesus' use of figurative language, prepare yourself to hear these expressions as fresh challenges to your heart, soul, and mind.

WE MUST BE BORN AGAIN

JOHN 3:3 NIV
*In reply Jesus declared, "I tell you the truth,
no one can see the kingdom of God
unless he is born again."*

No man can be truly united to the Church, so as to be reckoned among the children of God, until he has been previously renewed. This expression shows briefly what is the beginning of Christianity, and at the same time teaches us, that we are born exiles and utterly alienated from *the kingdom of God,* and that there is a perpetual state of variance between God and us, until he makes us altogether different by our being *born again;* for the statement is general, and comprehends the whole human race. If Christ had said to one person, or to a few individuals, that they could not *enter into heaven, unless they had been* previously *born again,* we might have supposed that it was only certain characters that were pointed out, but he speaks of all without exception; for the language is unlimited, and is of the same import with such universal terms as these: *Whosoever shall not be born again cannot enter into the kingdom of God.*

JOHN CALVIN

THE FOUNTAIN OF GOD

JOHN 3:4 ESV

Nicodemus said to him, "How can a man be born when he is old? Can he enter a second time into his mother's womb and be born?"

The power of divine wisdom is so great that, when infused into one's heart, it expels foolishness (the mother of all fault) by one impulse—once and for all. This wisdom doesn't need payment, books, or nightly studies to come about. But the results are accomplished freely, easily, and quickly, if only ears are open and the heart thirsts for wisdom. Don't be afraid: we don't sell water or offer the sun as a reward. The fountain of God, most abundant and full, is open to everyone. This heavenly light rises for everyone who has eyes. Did the philosophers bring about these things, or can they accomplish these results if they want? For although they spend their lives studying philosophy, they can neither improve any person nor improve themselves. . . . Their wisdom at its best doesn't eradicate, but actually hides faults. However, a few of God's principles will change people so completely and make them new by having them put off their old selves so that you wouldn't recognize them as the same.

LACTANTIUS

THE WONDER OF GOD'S LOVE

JOHN 3:5-6 NIV
Jesus answered, "I tell you the truth, no one can enter the kingdom of God unless he is born of water and the Spirit. Flesh gives birth to flesh, but the Spirit gives birth to spirit."

It sounds crazy, as it did to Nicodemus, an early intellectual and a potential BBC panelist who asked how in the world it was possible for someone already born to go back into the womb and be born again. It happens. It has happened innumerable times. It goes on happening. The testimony to this effect is overwhelming. Suddenly to be caught up in the wonder of God's love flooding the universe, made aware of the stupendous creativity which animates all life, of our own participation in it, every colour brighter, every meaning clearer. . . . Above all, every human face, all human companionship, all human encounters, recognizably a family affair. . . . This is a fulfillment that transcends all human fulfilling and yet is accessible to all humans, based on the absolutes of love rather than the relativities of justice, on the universality of brotherhood rather than the particularity of equality, on the perfect service which is freedom rather than the perfect servitude which purports to be freedom.

MALCOLM MUGGERIDGE

THE COST

JOHN 3:7–8 NRSV

*"Do not be astonished that I said to you,
'You must be born from above.' The wind blows
where it chooses, and you hear the sound of it,
but you do not know where it comes from
or where it goes. So it is with everyone
who is born of the Spirit."*

Occasionally you hear people talking about the cost of becoming a Christian; then in the next breath they will tell you that salvation is free! "Eternal life is a gift, but there is a price to pay," they exclaim. . . .

I think a better way of looking at it would be to realize that there is a price, but it has been completely paid—by Christ. Having paid the price of our ransom from sin with his death on the cross, Christ rose again to offer us life through a relationship with him. Eternal life is based absolutely on him. If there is no relationship, there is no eternal life.

Obviously, if eternal life is based on a relationship to him, then he is perfectly entitled to state the terms of the relationship. His terms are quite straightforward: He is Lord, and therefore eternal life is a relationship that involves acknowledging his lordship. That isn't the cost so much as it is purely an elementary aspect of the relationship.

JILL AND STUART BRISCOE

EXAMINING THE WORD

JAMES 1:18 ESV
*Of his own will he brought us forth by
the word of truth, that we should be
a kind of firstfruits of his creatures.*

The point that James is making in this verse is that *God
brought Christians to birth through the Word*. . . . As
born-again children, Christians are the first fruits of creation—that part which is given to God to be his sole
possession and to be partaker of his holiness. These are the
dimensions of the new dignity and destiny into which the
Word introduces us.

In verse 21 James goes on to say that *God brings people
to glory through the Word*. Everything depends on our being
"quick to hear" and receive the Word with meekness, so
that it becomes "implanted" in the soil of our hearts. . . .

In verse 25 we see that *God blesses those who are doers of
the Word*. A religion of hearing and not doing is hypocrisy
and self-deceit. To forget the needs which God's message
exposes is frivolous, stupid, and inexcusable. To look at
the Word closely, and to persevere in doing what it says,
is the only way to be blessed.

J. I. PACKER

MORE RIGHTEOUS
THAN THE PHARISEES

MATTHEW 5:20 NLT

*"But I warn you—unless you obey God better than
the teachers of religious law and the Pharisees do,
you can't enter the Kingdom of Heaven at all!"*

The scribes and Pharisees venerated, studied, and ex-
pounded the Law of God—or so they thought. . . .
They supposed that the Law had only to do with behavior patterns, being thus like traffic regulations or an indus-
trial rule book, and that keeping it meant no more than
conforming to these outward patterns and rules.

But Jesus challenges the narrow Pharisaic understanding of the law's requirements. He overthrows the external
rule—the righteousness which the Jewish religious leaders practiced—and replaces it with a righteousness which
is of the Spirit as well as the letter and starts in the heart
before it finds expression in the life.

This righteousness will only be found in those who
have been born again. . . . The righteousness he requires
reflects God's heart and character, and such behavior cannot issue from our own heart and character till we are
born of and animated by the Holy Spirit.

J. I. PACKER

THE MYSTERY OF GRACE

ROMANS 8:5–6 NLT
*Those who are dominated by the sinful nature
think about sinful things, but those who are
controlled by the Holy Spirit think about things
that please the Spirit. If your sinful nature controls
your mind, there is death. But if the Holy Spirit
controls your mind, there is life and peace.*

Paul divides people into two categories—those who
let themselves be controlled by their sinful natures,
and those who follow after the Holy Spirit. All of us
would be in the first category if Jesus hadn't offered us a
way out. Once we have said yes to Jesus, we will want to
continue following him, because his way brings life and
peace. Daily we must consciously choose to center our
lives on God. Use the Bible to discover God's guidelines,
and then follow them. In every perplexing situation ask
yourself, "What would Jesus want me to do?" When the
Holy Spirit points out what is right, do it eagerly.

LIFE APPLICATION BIBLE

THE VINEYARD

JOHN 15:1 NLT
*"I am the true vine,
and my Father is the gardener."*

In the Old Testament, God's people were often pictured as His vineyard. However, they were not always pictured as a fruitful vineyard. Hosea described Israel as a luxuriant vine, but without fruit (Hosea 10:1). Isaiah compared God's investment in Israel with a farmer who invests in a vineyard only to find that the fruit it produces is wild and bitter (Isaiah 5:1–7). . . .

Jesus declared Himself to be the true vine. Using the language of the vine grower, Jesus described a living union between His disciples and Himself. Just as Jesus is connected to the Father, all followers of Jesus are connected to the Father through their living fellowship with Jesus. The result of this living union is holiness and eternal life (Romans 6:22). His life flows into our lives and transforms, or changes us, into His likeness. His holiness changes our lives and makes us useful to God, as Jesus' life was useful to the Father.

HENRY BLACKABY AND ROY EDGEMON

THE TRUE VINE

JOHN 15:1 NKJV
*"I am the true vine,
and My Father is the vinedresser."*

I *am the true Vine.* The general meaning of this comparison is, that we are, by nature, barren and dry, except in so far as we have been ingrafted into Christ, and draw from him a power which is new, and which does not proceed from ourselves. . . .

There is scarcely any one who is ashamed to acknowledge that every thing good which he possesses comes from God; but, after making this acknowledgment, they imagine that a universal grace has been given to them, as if it had been implanted in them by nature. But Christ dwells principally on this, that the vital sap—that is, all life and strength—proceeds from himself alone. . . . When he calls himself *the* TRUE *vine,* the meaning is, I *am* TRULY *the vine,* and therefore men toil to no purpose in seeking strength anywhere else, for from none will useful fruit proceed but from *the branches* which shall be produced by me.

JOHN CALVIN

What Kind of Reflection Are You?

John 15:4–5 NLT

*"Remain in me, and I will remain in you.
For a branch cannot produce fruit if it is severed from
the vine, and you cannot be fruitful apart from me.
Yes, I am the vine; you are the branches. Those who
remain in me, and I in them, will produce much
fruit. For apart from me you can do nothing."*

Observe: "We are *changed*." The mistake we have
been making is that we have been trying to change
ourselves. That is not possible. . . . Now, the moment you
give that over into Christ's care—the moment you see
that you are *being* changed—that anxiety passes away. . . .

That is the way to get joy. It is to abide in Christ. Out
of this simple relationship we have faith, we have peace,
we have joy. Many other things follow. A man's usefulness
depends to a large extent upon his fellowship with Christ.
That is obvious. Only Christ can influence the world; but
all that the world sees of Christ is what it sees of you and
me. Christ said: "The world seeth Me no more, but ye see
Me." You see Him, and standing in front of Him, reflect
Him, and the world sees the reflection. It cannot see Him.
So that a Christian's usefulness depends solely upon that
relationship.

Henry Drummond

TAKE TIME TO BE QUIET

JOHN 15:4 ESV

"Abide in me, and I in you. As the branch cannot bear fruit by itself, unless it abides in the vine, neither can you, unless you abide in me."

The pace and preoccupations of urbanized, mechanized, collectivized, secularized modern life are such that any sort of inner life is very hard to maintain. To make prayer your life priority, as countless Christians of former days did outside as well as inside the monastery, is stupendously difficult in a world that runs you off your feet and will not let you slow down. And if you attempt it, you will certainly seem eccentric to your peers, for nowadays involvement in a stream of programmed activities is decidedly "in" and the older ideal of a quiet, contemplative life is just as decidedly "out."

That there is a widespread hunger today for more intimacy, warmth, and affection in our fellowship with God is clear from the current renewal of interest in the experiential writings of the Puritans and the contemplative tradition of prayer. . . . But the concept of the Christian life as sanctified rush and bustle still dominates, and as a result the experiential side of Christian holiness remains very much a closed book.

J. I. PACKER

HIDDEN WITH CHRIST

JOHN 15:4 NASB

*"Abide in Me, and I in you. As the branch cannot
bear fruit of itself unless it abides in the vine,
neither can you unless you abide in Me."*

Abiding in the Lord Jesus does not only mean trusting in Him. It includes yielding ourselves up to
Him to receive His life and letting that life work out its
results in us. We live in Him, by Him, for Him, to Him
when we abide in Him. We feel that all our separate life
has gone, for "ye are dead, and your life is hidden with
Christ in God" (Colossians 3:3). . . .

We have no reason for existence except in Christ, but
what a reason that is! The vine needs the branch as truly
as the branch needs the vine. No vine ever bore any fruit
except upon its branches. Truly it bears all the branches,
and so bears all the fruit, but yet it is by the branch that
the vine displays its fruitfulness. . . . Jesus said, "Every
branch in me that beareth fruit, he purgeth it" (John
15:2). Take care that you abide in Christ when you are
being purged.

C. H. SPURGEON

BEING KEPT BY GOD

JOHN 15:5–6 NRSV
"I am the vine, you are the branches.
Those who abide in me and I in them bear much fruit,
because apart from me you can do nothing.
Whoever does not abide in me is thrown away
like a branch and withers; such branches are gathered,
thrown into the fire, and burned."

Abiding in Jesus is not a work that needs each moment the mind to be engaged, or the affections to be directly and actively occupied with it. It is an entrusting of oneself to the keeping of the Eternal Love, in the faith that it will abide near us, and with its holy presence watch over us and ward off the evil, even when we have to be most intently occupied with other things. And so the heart has rest and peace and joy in the consciousness of being kept when it cannot keep itself.

ANDREW MURRAY

TRUST IN HIM

JOHN 15:9–10 NIV

"As the Father has loved me, so have I loved you.
Now remain in my love. If you obey my commands,
you will remain in my love, just as I have obeyed
my Father's commands and remain in his love."

When love is heard inviting more trust, more love, the encouragement to trust, to love, goes beyond the rebuke that our love is so little, and we take heart to confide in the love that is saying, "Give me thine heart," expecting that it will impart itself to us, and enable us to give the response of love which it desires. For indeed it must be with the blessed purpose to enable us to love Him that our God bids us love Him; for He knows that no love but what He Himself quickens in us can love Him.

Therefore always feel the *call* to love a gracious *promise* of strength to love, and marvel not at your own deadness, but trust in Him who quickeneth the dead.

JOHN McLEOD CAMPBELL

PLACE OF REST

JOHN 15:11 ESV
*"These things I have spoken to you, that my joy
may be in you, and that your joy may be full."*

My most useful method is this simple attention, and
such a general passionate regard to God, to whom
I find myself often attached with greater sweetness and
delight than that of an infant at the mother's breast; so
that, if I dare use the expression, I should choose to call
this state the bosom of God, for the inexpressible sweetness which I taste and experience there. . . .

As for my set hours of prayer, they are only a con-
tinuation of the same exercise. Sometimes I consider
myself there as a stone before a carver, whereof he is to
make a statue; presenting myself thus before God, I desire
Him to form His perfect image in my soul, and make me
entirely like Himself.

At other times, when I apply myself to prayer, I feel all
my spirit and all my soul lift itself up without any care or
effort of mine, and it continues as it were suspended and
firmly fixed in God, as in its center and place of rest.

BROTHER LAWRENCE

GOD ALONE

PHILIPPIANS 2:13 NASB
For it is God who is at work in you,
both to will and to work for His good pleasure.

One of the futile methods of sanctifying ourselves is trying effort—struggle—agonizing. I suppose you have all tried that, and I appeal to your own life when I ask if it has not failed. Crossing the Atlantic, the *Etruria,* in which I was sailing, suddenly stopped in mid-ocean—something had broken down. There were a thousand people on board that ship. Do you think we could have made it go if we had all gathered together and pushed against the sides or against the masts? When a man hopes to sanctify himself by trying, he is like a man trying to make the boat go that carries him by pushing it—he is like a man drowning in the water and trying to save himself by pulling the hair of his own head. It is impossible. Christ held up the mode of sanctification almost to ridicule when He said: "Which of you by taking thought can add a cubit to his stature?" Put down that method forever as futile.

HENRY DRUMMOND

SALT

MATTHEW 5:13 NKJV

*"You are the salt of the earth; but if the salt
loses its flavor, how shall it be seasoned?
It is then good for nothing but to be thrown
out and trampled underfoot by men."*

Ye are the salt." Jesus does not say: "You *must* be the
salt." It is not for the disciples to decide whether they
will be the salt of the earth, for they are so whether
they like it or not, they have been made salt by the call
they have received. . . .

Everything else can be saved by salt, however bad it has
gone—only salt which loses its savour has no hope of
recovery. That is the other side of the picture. That is the
judgement which always hangs over the disciple community, whose mission is to save the world, but which, if it
ceases to live up to that mission, is itself irretrievably lost.
The call of Jesus Christ means either that we are the salt
of the earth, or else we are annihilated; either we follow
the call or we are crushed beneath it. There is no question of a second chance.

DIETRICH BONHOEFFER

DON'T LOSE YOUR TANG

MATTHEW 5:13–14 NLT

*"You are the salt of the earth. But what good is salt
if it has lost its flavor? Can you make it useful again?
It will be thrown out and trampled underfoot as
worthless. You are the light of the world—like a city
on a mountain, glowing in the night for all to see."*

Salt preserves what would otherwise rot and gives flavor to what would otherwise be flavorless; also, salt creates thirst. So Christians by the quality of their lives and by their actions should restrain evil and keep society from rotting, add savor to community life by, among other things, doing right and treating people with respect, and stir up a thirst for God.

Jesus is really telling his disciples to be what they are: You are salt, he says. Now be it! You're not living by the same scale of values as the rest of men, and people should notice this as they watch you in your homes, in your work, in the wider world. Don't lose your "tang." Be uncompromisingly different. Again, you are the light of the world. Be what you are: a source of illumination, guidance, and hope to all around you.

J. I. PACKER

PRESERVED TO THE END

MATTHEW 5:13 NASB
*"You are the salt of the earth; but if the salt has
become tasteless, how can it be made salty again?
It is no longer good for anything, except to be
thrown out and trampled under foot by men."*

The salt of the earth, I suppose, seems at first like nothing special. So what did Jesus mean when he called the apostles the "salt of the earth"? We must look for the words' appropriate meaning. Both the apostles' task and the nature of salt itself will reveal this. The element of water and the element of fire are combined and united in salt. So ordinary salt, made for the use of the human race, imparts resistance to corruption to the meats on which it is sprinkled. And, of course, it is very apt to add the sensation of hidden flavor. Like sowers, they sow immortality on all bodies on which their discourse has been sprinkled. They are perfected by the baptism of water and fire. So those who are to be salted with the power of gospel teaching have rightly been called the "salt of the earth." They are right now being preserved to the end.

HILARY OF POITIERS

THE PURPOSE OF SALT

MATTHEW 5:16–17 NIV

*"In the same way, let your light shine before men,
that they may see your good deeds and praise your
Father in heaven. Do not think that I have come
to abolish the Law or the Prophets; I have not
come to abolish them but to fulfill them."*

God has chosen you, in order to remove, through
you, the wavering from the rest of men; through
you the peoples are to be, as it were, preserved from corruption. Therefore, insipid salt *'is of no use but to be thrown
out and trodden underfoot by men.'* Consequently, the one
who is trodden underfoot by men is not the man who
suffers persecution, but the man who becomes foolish by
fearing persecution. No one can be trodden underfoot
unless he is underneath, and a man is not underneath if
his heart is fixed in heaven, even though he may be
enduring many bodily evils on earth.

'You are the light of the world.' . . . In this present sentence
we are to understand that the term, *'world,'* does not
denote the earth and the sky, but that it denotes the men
who are in the world or those who love the world—men
for whose enlightenment the Apostles have been sent.
'A city set on a mountain cannot be hidden.'

AUGUSTINE

WITNESSING TO OTHERS

MARK 16:15 NLT
And then he told them, "Go into all the world and preach the Good News to everyone, everywhere."

Nothing is more frigid than a Christian who does not care about the salvation of others. You cannot plead the excuse of poverty here; the widow who gave her two mites will stand to accuse you. Peter said, "Silver or gold I have none." Paul was so poor he often went hungry, lacking necessary food. You cannot plead lowliness. They were of low estate and so were their parents. You cannot allege lack of education or preparation. They were unlearned men. You cannot plead infirmity. Timothy was often laid low by sickness and the Apostle had to counsel him to take a little wine for his stomach. Every one can profit his neighbor if he will do what he can.

. . . This witnessing to others is part of the very nature of being a Christian. It would be easier for the sun to cease to shine and give forth heat than for a Christian not to send forth light; easier for the light to be darkness than for this to be so.

JOHN CHRYSOSTOM

LOOK UP AND OUT!

COLOSSIANS 3:12–13 ESV
Put on then, as God's chosen ones, holy and beloved,
compassion, kindness, humility, meekness, and patience,
bearing with one another and, if one has a complaint
against another, forgiving each other; as the Lord
has forgiven you, so you also must forgive.

Self-preoccupation, self-broodings, self-interest, self-love—these are the reasons why you go jarring against your fellows. Turn your eyes off yourself; look up, and out! There are men, your brothers, and women, your sisters; they have needs that you can aid. Listen for their confidences; keep your heart wide open to their calls, and your hands alert for their service. Learn to give, and not to take; to drown your own hungry wants in the happiness of lending yourself to fulfil the interests of those nearest or dearest. Look up and out, from this narrow, cabined self of yours, and you will jar no longer; you will fret no more, you will provoke no more; but you will, to your own glad surprise, find the secret of "the meekness and the gentleness of Jesus;" and the fruits of the Spirit will all bud and blossom from out of your life.

HENRY SCOTT HOLLAND

WORKERS WITH GOD

EPHESIANS 4:15–16 NIV

*Instead, speaking the truth in love, we will in all
things grow up into him who is the Head, that is,
Christ. From him the whole body, joined and held
together by every supporting ligament, grows and
builds itself up in love, as each part does its work.*

We become the living means to a great end; and all
our inner salvation—our finding of Jesus—is
seen, not to centre in ourselves, in our own gain, our own
rescue, our own peace; but to lead out beyond itself; to
have been our qualification for use and office, without
which we could not be taken up, as workers with God,
into that eternal husbandry whereby He sets Himself to
win over the stubborn and thorny field of the world. Our
eyes are taken off ourselves; we are not absorbed in
rehearsing our own experiences, however blessed. We are
caught up into the counsels; we serve to widen the fron-
tiers of the Kingdom; through us, correlated as we are, by
joints and bands, into the articulated body, the Spirit of
Christ can get abroad, can take a fresh step forward. We
are become its vantage-ground from which it can again
advance. Oh, that we were more quick to His touch,
more ready for His needs, more serviceable in His ministry!

HENRY SCOTT HOLLAND

WAIT UPON GOD

MATTHEW 11:29 NKJV
"Take My yoke upon you and learn from Me,
for I am gentle and lowly in heart,
and you will find rest for your souls."

We must learn of Jesus, how He is meek and lowly of heart. He teaches us where true humility takes its rise and finds its strength—in the knowledge that it is God who worketh all in all, that our place is to yield to Him in perfect resignation and dependence, in full consent to be and to do nothing of ourselves. This is the life Christ came to reveal and to impart—a life to God that came through death to sin and self. . . . The root of all virtue and grace, of all faith and acceptable worship, is that we know that we have nothing but what we receive, and bow in deepest humility to wait upon God for it.

ANDREW MURRAY

PICTURES OF
JESUS' ROLE

*"Whoever believes in me, as the Scripture
has said, streams of living water
will flow from within him."*
JOHN 7:38 NIV

PICTURES OF JESUS' ROLE

Volumes have been written about Jesus' titles and roles. His titles (Lord, Savior, Christ, King, etc.) convey a sense of His authority, majesty, and divine nature. His role names (Bread, Shepherd, Door, Vine, and others) convey His actions, particularly in relationship to us, those He came to seek and to save. These role names are simple, unexpected, and rich in significance. Often, a few moments of insight into the surrounding culture of Jesus' time make His words leap off the page and transform our lives. They help us see and feel Christ's work on our behalf. They fill our environment with "labeled" items that remind us of Jesus.

As you savor these readings on Jesus' role names, think about how each of them widens and deepens your understanding of what Christ has done and is doing for you.

STAND FIRM

MATTHEW 7:13–14 NIV

*"Enter through the narrow gate. For wide is the gate
and broad is the road that leads to destruction, and
many enter through it. But small is the gate and narrow
the road that leads to life, and only a few find it."*

What is it that makes the way so narrow and hard?
None other than the devil himself, the world,
and our own lazy flesh. It is resistant and defensive, and it
refuses to go on trusting God and clinging to His Word.
It cannot stand poverty, danger, and the contempt of the
world. In other words, it would like to travel on the wide
road. Therefore it makes this road distasteful and hard for
us. Next comes the world, with its persecution, hanging,
murder, fire, and drowning, all because we refuse to travel
on the wide way with it. If there is nothing else it can do,
it venomously slanders and disgraces us, hounding us with
sword, fire, and water. . . . And then comes the devil himself. He tortures the heart with evil thoughts of unbelief,
fear, dread, and despair. Everything good that we do he
turns into sin and shame. Surrounded by such enemies,
we are still supposed to stand firm and to keep our goal
in mind.

MARTIN LUTHER

THE YOKE OF THE LORD

MATTHEW 7:13−14 NASB
*"Enter through the narrow gate; for the gate is wide
and the way is broad that leads to destruction,
and there are many who enter through it.
For the gate is small and the way is narrow
that leads to life, and there are few who find it."*

Jesus Christ said to all Christians without exception,
"Let him who would be my disciple carry his cross, and
follow me." The broad way leads to perdition. We must
follow the narrow way which few enter. We must be
born again, renounce ourselves, hate ourselves, become a
child, be poor in spirit, weep to be comforted, and not be
of the world which is cursed because of its scandals.

These truths frighten many people, and this is because
they only know what religion exacts without knowing
what it offers, and they ignore the spirit of love which
makes everything easy. They do not know that it leads to
the highest perfection by a feeling of peace and love
which sweetens all the struggle.

Those who are wholly God's are always happy. They
know by experience that the yoke of the Lord is "easy
and light," that we find in him "rest for the soul," and that
he comforts those who are weary and overburdened, as
he himself has said.

FRANÇOIS FÉNELON

THE NARROW ROAD

MATTHEW 7:13–14 NLT
*"You can enter God's Kingdom only through
the narrow gate. The highway to hell is broad,
and its gate is wide for the many who choose
the easy way. But the gateway to life is small,
and the road is narrow, and only a few ever find it."*

The path of discipleship is narrow, and it is fatally easy
to miss one's way and stray from the path, even after
years of discipleship. And it is hard to find. On either side
of the narrow path deep chasms yawn. To be called to a
life of extraordinary quality, to live up to it, and yet to be
unconscious of it is indeed a narrow way. . . . If we worry
about the dangers that beset us, if we gaze at the road
instead of at him who goes before, we are already straying
from the path. For he is himself the way, the narrow way
and the strait gate. . . . The very narrowness of the road
will increase our certainty. The way which the Son of
God trod on earth, and the way which we too must tread
as citizens of two worlds on the razor edge between this
world and the kingdom of heaven, could hardly be a
broad way. The narrow way is bound to be right.

DIETRICH BONHOEFFER

BE ON THE LOOKOUT

MATTHEW 7:14 KJV
*Because strait is the gate,
and narrow is the way,
which leadeth unto life,
and few there be that find it.*

Our dear Lord has now finished preaching. Finally He closes this sermon with several warnings, to arm us against all kinds of hindrances and offenses of both doctrine and life that we confront in the world. . . . Our dear Lord has in mind here that people may find it appealing and think to themselves: "I would like to live that way, but it takes a great deal." Christ says: "That is what I am saying, too. Therefore I am warning you to be on the lookout and not to let yourself be turned aside if it is a little sour and difficult, for it cannot be and will not be any other way in the world." A Christian has to know this and be armed against it, so that he does not let it trouble him or hinder him if the whole world lives otherwise.

MARTIN LUTHER

THE GIFT OF SIGHT

JOHN 8:12 NKJV
Then Jesus spoke to them again, saying,
"I am the light of the world.
He who follows Me shall not walk in darkness,
but have the light of life."

We, whose spiritual eyes have been opened by the Word, Jesus Christ, and who see the difference between light and darkness, prefer to take our stand "in the light." We won't have anything at all to do with darkness. In addition, the true Light, endowed with life, knows who to reveal His full splendor to and to whom His light. For He doesn't just display His brilliance due to the weakness in the recipient's eyes. And whose eyes are affected and injured if we must speak of them at all? Those who are ignorant of God and whose passions prevent them from seeing the truth. Christians, however, aren't blinded by the words of those who opposed worshiping God. But let those who know they are blinded by following crowds who are in error and groups that keep festivals to demons, draw near to the Word, Jesus Christ. He can give the gift of sight.

ORIGEN

DAILY FAITH

JOHN 8:12 NASB

Then Jesus again spoke to them, saying,
"I am the Light of the world;
he who follows Me will not walk in the darkness,
but will have the Light of life."

It is vitally important that we hold the truth of God's infinite wisdom as a tenet of our creed; but this is not enough. We must by the exercise of faith and by prayer bring it into the practical world of our day-by-day experience.

To believe actively that our Heavenly Father constantly spreads around us providential circumstances that work for our present good and our everlasting well-being brings to the soul a veritable benediction. Most of us go through life praying a little, planning a little, jockeying for position, hoping but never being quite certain of anything. . . .

There is a better way. It is to repudiate our own wisdom and take instead the infinite wisdom of God. Our insistence upon seeing ahead is natural enough, but it is a real hindrance to our spiritual progress. God has charged Himself with full responsibility for our eternal happiness and stands ready to take over the management of our lives the moment we turn in faith to Him.

A. W. TOZER

THE POWER OF THE WORD

JOHN 8:12 NLT

Jesus said to the people, "I am the light of the world.
If you follow me, you won't be stumbling
through the darkness, because you will have
the light that leads to life."

So was I speaking and weeping in the most bitter contrition of my heart, when, lo! I heard from a neighbouring house a voice, as of boy or girl, I know not, chanting, and oft repeating, "Take up and read; take up and read." Instantly, my countenance altered. . . . Checking the torrent of my tears, I arose; interpreting it to be no other than a command from God to open the book, and read the first chapter I should find. . . .

I seized, opened, and in silence read that section on which my eyes first fell: Not in rioting and drunkenness, not in chambering and wantonness, not in strife and envying; but put ye on the Lord Jesus Christ, and make not provision for the flesh, in concupiscence [Romans 13:13–14]. No further would I read; nor needed I: for instantly at the end of this sentence, by a light as it were of serenity infused into my heart, all the darkness of doubt vanished away.

AUGUSTINE

ONE DOOR

JOHN 10:7 KJV
Then said Jesus unto them again, Verily, verily,
I say unto you, I am the door of the sheep.

I am the door. . . . The head of all spiritual teaching, which souls are fed on, consists in Him. Hence also Paul, one of the shepherds, says, 'I thought nothing worth knowing save Jesus Christ' (I Corinthians 2:12). And this expression is equivalent to Christ saying that it is to Him alone that we must all be gathered together. He therefore invites and exhorts all who desire salvation, to come to Himself. By these words He means that those who have left Him and still strive after God, wander about in vain, since only one door lies open and every other approach is barred. . . .

In short, Christ says that all the doctrines which have led the world away from Him are deadly plagues, since apart from Him is nothing but destruction and a horrible scattering. . . . What should be considered is that there is only one door and that those who bypass it and make openings or breaches in the walls are thieves.

JOHN CALVIN

SHEPHERDS IN THE CHURCH

JOHN 10:11 KJV
I am the good shepherd:
the good shepherd giveth his life for the sheep.

The good shepherd giveth *His life for the sheep.* From the extraordinary affection which He bears towards the *sheep,* He shows how truly He acts towards them as a *shepherd;* for He is so anxious about their salvation, that He does not even spare His own life. Hence it follows, that they who reject the guardianship of so kind and amiable a *shepherd* are exceedingly ungrateful, and deserve a hundred deaths, and are exposed to every kind of harm. . . . Nothing is more desirable than that the Church should be governed by good and diligent *shepherds.* Christ declares that *He is the good shepherd,* who keeps His Church safe and sound, first, by Himself, and, next, by His agents. Whenever there is good order, and fit men hold the government, then Christ shows that He is actually *the shepherd.* But there are many wolves and thieves who, wearing the garb of *shepherds,* wickedly scatter the Church. Whatever name such persons may assume, Christ threatens that we must avoid them.

JOHN CALVIN

RECEIVE THE LOST

JOHN 10:11 NIV

"I am the good shepherd. The good shepherd lays down his life for the sheep."

Christ, who is the good Shepherd, goes in quest of one who wanders and is lost in the mountains. He calls this one back when it runs from Him, and when He has found it, troubles Himself to carry it on His shoulders. But we, on the other hand, harshly reject such a shepherd when He approaches us. . . . When people set about doing evil or good to others, what they do doesn't just affect other people. Instead, depending on whether they attach themselves to wickedness or goodness, they themselves become controlled either by godly virtues or by unbridled passions. The former become the followers and friends of good angels. . . . But the latter will immediately fall away from the peace of God and from peace with themselves. Both in this world and after death, they will dwell with the murderous spirits. Therefore, don't reject those who want to return in repentance. Instead, receive the lost gladly, count them again among the faithful, and make up what is defective in them.

DIONYSIUS OF ALEXANDRIA

THE SHEPHERD OF SHEPHERDS

JOHN 10:12 NIV

*"The hired hand is not the shepherd who owns
the sheep. So when he sees the wolf coming,
he abandons the sheep and runs away.
Then the wolf attacks the flock and scatters it."*

Watch out! The wolf doesn't attack the Lord's flock
stealthily at night anymore, but in open daylight.
We see him move toward slaughtering the sheep, yet we
oppose him without caution and without darts of words.
. . . We must study to make our hearts passionate by imitating earthly shepherds. They often keep watch through
winter nights, nipped by rain and frost, lest even one
sheep should perish. And if the prowler does bite one
greedily, they busy themselves to save it. They pant with
rapid heartbeats, leap to rescue the sheep with loud cries,
and are stimulated by the urgency, lest the lord of the
flock require what they lost carelessly. Watch then, lest
anything perish. And if anything is seized by chance,
bring it back to the Lord's flock by cries of godly instruction. Then the Shepherd of shepherds may mercifully
approve of us in His judgment for having watched over
His flock.

GREGORY I

JESUS SEES DIFFERENTLY

JOHN 10:11–12 NLT

*"I am the good shepherd. The good shepherd lays
down his life for the sheep. A hired hand will run
when he sees a wolf coming. He will leave the sheep
because they aren't his and he isn't their shepherd.
And so the wolf attacks them and scatters the flock."*

The Good Shepherd protects his sheep against the
wolf, and instead of fleeing he gives his life for the
sheep. He knows them all by name and loves them.
He knows their distress and their weakness. He heals
the wounded, gives drink to the thirsty, sets upright the
falling, and leads them gently, not sternly, to pasture. . . .

From the human point of view everything looks hope-
less, but Jesus sees things with different eyes. Instead of
the people maltreated, wretched and poor, he sees the
ripe harvest field of God. "The harvest is great." It is ripe
enough to be gathered into the barns. . . .

There is now no time to lose: the work of harvest
brooks no delay. "But the labourers are few." It is hardly
surprising that so few are granted to see things with the
pitying eyes of Jesus, for only those who share the love of
his heart have been given eyes to see. And only they can
enter the harvest field.

DIETRICH BONHOEFFER

HE WILL SUSTAIN US

ISAIAH 40:11 ESV
He will tend his flock like a shepherd;
he will gather the lambs in his arms;
he will carry them in his bosom,
and gently lead those that are with young.

Feed us, Your children, as sheep. Master, fill us with righteousness from Your own pasture. Instructor, give us food on Your holy mountain, the church, which towers in the air, is above the clouds, and touches heaven. "And I will be," He says, "their Shepherd," and will be as near to them as clothes to their skin. He wants to save my flesh by enveloping it in the robe of immortality, and He has anointed my body. . . . We who are passing over to eternal life will not fall into corruption because He will sustain us. For so He has said and so He has willed. Our Instructor is righteously good. "I came not," He says, "to be ministered unto, but to minister." Therefore, He is introduced in the Gospel as "wearied," because He toiled for us and promised "to give His life as a ransom for many."

CLEMENT OF ALEXANDRIA

WATCH CAREFULLY

JOHN 10:12–14 NKJV
"But a hireling, he who is not the shepherd,
one who does not own the sheep, sees the wolf
coming and leaves the sheep and flees; and the wolf
catches the sheep and scatters them. The hireling flees
because he is a hireling and does not care about
the sheep. I am the good shepherd; and I know
My sheep, and am known by My own."

The devil's attacks are frequent and fierce and he sur-
rounds our salvation on all sides. Therefore, we must
watch and be sober. We must fortify ourselves against his
assault. For if he gains even a slight advantage, he will
enter in easily and introduce all his forces to a great
degree. So then, if we care about our salvation at all, we
must not allow him to even approach slightly, but must
restrain him in important matters beforehand. . . . If such
wounds were sensible, or the body had received the
blows, we could easily discern his plots. But since the soul
is what receives the wounds and is invisible, we all need
to watch carefully. For no one knows a person's heart as
well as that person's own spirit. For the Word is spoken to
everyone and is offered as a general remedy to anyone
who needs it. But each individual hearer must accept the
remedy that is appropriate for his own ailments.

JOHN CHRYSOSTOM

Forget Yourself

Galatians 2:20 NASB

*I have been crucified with Christ; and it is no longer
I who live, but Christ lives in me; and the life which
I now live in the flesh I live by faith in the Son of
God, who loved me and gave Himself up for me.*

The transformation of our lives by the Holy Spirit,
which St. Paul calls the renewal of the mind, is the
real beginning of life but foreign to pagan philosophers.
These philosophers set up reason as the sole guide of life,
of wisdom and conduct. But Christian philosophy
demands of us that we surrender our reason to the Holy
Spirit. This means that we no longer live for ourselves,
but that Christ lives and reigns within us (Ephesians 4:23;
Galatians 2:20).

Let us therefore not seek our own, but that which
pleases the Lord and is helpful to the promotion of his
glory. There is a great advantage in almost forgetting ourselves and in surely neglecting all selfish aspects; for then
only can we try faithfully to devote our attention to God
and his commandments.

John Calvin

WHEN I LOVE GOD

JOHN 6:32–33 ESV

*Jesus then said to them, "Truly, truly, I say to you,
it was not Moses who gave you the bread from heaven,
but my Father gives you the true bread from heaven.
For the bread of God is he who comes down
from heaven and gives life to the world."*

I love You, Lord, not with uncertainty, but consciously and with certainty. . . . But what do I love in loving You? Not physical beauty, the splendor of time, or the pleasant radiance of light. Not the sweet melodies of all kinds of songs or the fragrant smell of flowers, ointments, and spices. Not manna and honey. Not limbs that are pleasant for fleshly embraces. I don't love these things when I love my God. Yet, I love a certain kind of light, sound, fragrance, food, and embrace in loving my God. He is the light, sound, fragrance, food, and embrace of my inner person. In this love, the light shines that can't be contained into my soul. It is where those things resound that time can't snatch away, where there is a fragrance that no breeze can scatter, where there is a food which no amount of eating can cut into, and where there is a clinging to that no gratification can break apart. This is what I love when I love my God.

AUGUSTINE

THE NAMES OF JESUS

JOHN 6:35 ESV
Jesus said to them, "I am the bread of life;
whoever comes to me shall not hunger,
and whoever believes in me shall never thirst."

It is no wonder that Jesus is named after many good things in the Gospel. If we look at the names by which the Son of God is called, we will understand how many of these good things He is. The feet of those who preach His name are beautiful. One good thing is life. Jesus is the Life. Another good thing is the light of the world (when it is true light that enlightens people). And the Son of God is said to be all these things. . . . Ah, isn't it good that the Lord shook off earth and mortality to rise again? And we have obtained this benefit from the Lord: that He is the Resurrection. . . . We must not neglect mentioning the Word, who is God after the Father of all. For this another good, no less than the others. Happy, then, are those who accept these goods and receive them from those who announce their blessings, those whose feet are beautiful.

ORIGEN

THE EXCELLENCY OF CHRIST

JOHN 6:35 NLT

*Jesus replied, "I am the bread of life. No one
who comes to me will ever be hungry again.
Those who believe in me will never thirst."*

The excellency of Christ is such, that the discovery
of it is exceedingly contenting and satisfying to the
soul. . . .

This excellency of Jesus Christ is the suitable food of
the rational soul. The soul that comes to Christ, feeds
upon this, and lives upon it; it is that bread which came
down from heaven, of which he that eats shall not die; it
is angels' food, it is that wine and milk that is given without money, and without price. This is that fatness in
which the believing soul delights itself; here the longing
soul may be satisfied, and the hungry soul may be filled
with goodness. The delight and contentment that is to
be found here, passeth understanding, and is unspeakable and full of glory. It is impossible for those who have
tasted of this fountain, and know the sweetness of it, ever
to forsake it. The soul has found the river of water of life,
and it desires no other drink; it has found the tree of
life, and it desires no other fruit.

JONATHAN EDWARDS

HIS BLOOD AND BODY

JOHN 6:48–50 NIV

*"I am the bread of life. Your forefathers ate the manna
in the desert, yet they died.
But here is the bread that comes down from heaven,
which a man may eat and not die."*

Human beings are the only members of God's creatures in this world who do not give their life as
material food to another creature. Humans are at the top
of the food chain. But not so spiritually. God sent God's
only Son, the Word, united with the man Jesus, to be our
spiritual food. By his life-giving death, Jesus poured out
the life of his body, his blood, so that his blood and body
does for us what we cannot do for ourselves—Jesus does
relationship for us with God. . . . By ingesting bread and
wine, we take into ourselves the life-giving sacrifice of
Jesus through whom death is conquered. Bread and wine,
eaten and drunk in faith, is the reality of receiving God's
life within, through which we are spiritually and physi-
cally nourished and sustained. Bread and wine is creation
becoming incarnation so that we may become re-
creation.

ROBERT E. WEBBER

THE BREAD OF LIFE

JOHN 6:35 NKJV
And Jesus said to them, "I am the bread of life.
He who comes to Me shall never hunger,
and he who believes in Me shall never thirst."

What oxygen is to the body, the Bread of Life is to the soul. Without that bread, all other hungers will be improperly perceived. . . . Life is meant to be lived with the fulfillment of the one need that defines all other means of fulfillment and the one love that defines all other loves. . . .

The people ought to have grasped more than they did. You see, to the Middle Eastern mind-set, bread is not just a source of nourishment. It is the bearer of so much more. Food is the means of fellowship. Jesus says, in Revelation 3:20, that He stands at the door and knocks; if anyone opens that door, He will come in and eat with him. What a beautiful expression that is of friendship. Food is the means of celebration. The return of the prodigal was celebrated by the killing of the fatted calf, which signaled that the feast had begun. Food is also a medium of pleasure. Solomon's palace thrived on such offerings. To this day, food is a big thing in eastern culture. As well as providing nourishment, it is the means of friendship, celebration, and pleasure.

RAVI ZACHARIAS

WE CANNOT COMPREHEND HIM

1 TIMOTHY 1:17 ESV

To the King of ages, immortal, invisible, the only God,
be honor and glory forever and ever. Amen.

No matter what knowledge of God we can gain by observing or reflecting on Him, He is far better than how we perceive Him. Say we wanted to acquaint someone who couldn't bear a spark of light or the flame of a very small lamp with the brightness and splendor of the sun. Wouldn't it be necessary to tell him that the sun's splendor was unspeakably and incalculably more glorious than all the light he had already seen? In the same way, our knowledge of God is restrained by flesh and blood. Due to our participation in material things, our minds are dull in their attempts to understand spiritual things, although our understanding hardly compares to a spark or lamp. However, among all intelligent, spiritual beings, God is superior to all others—so unspeakably and incalculably superior. Even the purest and brightest human understanding can't comprehend His nature.

ORIGEN

ALL FOR CHRIST

JOHN 6:51 NASB

*"I am the living bread that came down out
of heaven; if anyone eats of this bread, he will
live forever; and the bread also which I will
give for the life of the world is My flesh."*

Second, the fellowship acknowledges that all earthly
gifts are given to it only for Christ's sake, as this whole
world is sustained only for the sake of Jesus Christ, his
Word, and his message. He is the true bread of life. He is
not only the giver but the gift itself, for whose sake all
earthly gifts exist. Only because the message concerning
Jesus Christ must still go forth and find believers, and
because our task is not yet perfected, does God in His
patience continue to sustain us with His good gifts. So
the Christian table fellowship prays, in Luther's words:
"O Lord God, heavenly Father, bless unto us these Thy
gifts, which of Thy tender kindness Thou hast bestowed
upon us, through Jesus Christ our Lord. . . ." thus confessing that Jesus Christ is the divine Mediator and
Saviour.

DIETRICH BONHOEFFER

COME CLEAN

JOHN 6:54–56 NKJV

*"Whoever eats My flesh and drinks My blood
has eternal life, and I will raise him up at the
last day. For My flesh is food indeed, and My
blood is drink indeed. He who eats My flesh and
drinks My blood abides in Me, and I in him."*

Now, finally, He explains how what He is saying happens and what it is to eat His body and to drink
His blood. "He who eats my flesh and drinks my blood,
abides in me and I in him." Therefore, to eat that food
and to drink that drink is to abide in Christ and to have
Him abiding in oneself. And, as a result, he who does not
abide in Christ and in whom Christ does not abide,
beyond doubt neither eats His flesh nor drinks His blood,
but rather eats and drinks the sacrament of so great a thing
to judgment for himself, because he presumed to approach
unclean to the sacraments of Christ which one takes
worthily only if he is clean. And about these it is said,
"Blessed are the clean of heart, for they shall see God."

AUGUSTINE

FOLLOW HIM

JOHN 14:6 NIV
*Jesus answered, "I am the way and the truth
and the life. No one comes to the Father
except through me."*

My dear friend, the more you can leave yourself
behind, the more you will be able to enter into
me. Just as longing for nothing outside of yourself makes
for inner peace, so does letting go of yourself unite you
with God. I want you to learn to abandon yourself perfectly to my will, without grumbling or complaining.

Follow me. I am the Way, the Truth, and the Life. . . .

If you continue in my way you will know the truth,
and the truth will set you free. You will have eternal life.
If you wish to enter into life, keep the commandments.
If you wish to know the truth, believe in me. If you wish
to be perfect, sell all that you have. . . . If you wish to be
exalted in heaven, humble yourself in this world. If you
wish to reign with me, carry my cross, for only the servants of the cross find the road of blessedness and true
light.

THOMAS À KEMPIS

HIS DIVINE LOVE AND MERCY

1 CORINTHIANS 1:30 NLT
*God alone made it possible for you to be in
Christ Jesus. For our benefit God made Christ
to be wisdom itself. He is the one who made us
acceptable to God. He made us pure and holy,
and he gave himself to purchase our freedom.*

Blessed Lord Jesus,
Before thy cross I kneel and see
the heinousness of my sin,
my iniquity that caused thee to be 'made a curse'. . . .
Show me the enormity of my guilt by
the crown of thorns,
the pierced hands and feet, the bruised body,
the dying cries.
Thy blood is the blood of incarnate God,
its worth infinite, its value beyond all thought. . . .
Yet thy compassions yearn over me,
thy heart hastens to my rescue,
thy love endured my curse,
thy mercy bore my deserved stripes.
Let me walk humbly in the lowest depths of humiliation,
bathed in thy blood,
tender of conscience,
triumphing gloriously as an heir of salvation.

UNKNOWN

JESUS SURPASSES ALL

JOHN 4:7–9 NIV

When a Samaritan woman came to draw water,
Jesus said to her, "Will you give me a drink?"
(His disciples had gone into the town to buy food.)
The Samaritan woman said to him, "You are a Jew
and I am a Samaritan woman. How can you ask me for
a drink?" (For Jews do not associate with Samaritans.)

The Christ of God proclaims good news to prostitutes and tax collectors, to those caught up in squalid choices and failed dreams. He is Pantocrator (ruler of all), the creator and sovereign of the cosmos, above all powers, kings, thrones, and dominations. The star Upsilon Andromedae, positioned 264 trillion miles from Planet Earth, was created through him and for him. . . .

Jesus is not merely a super-human being with an intellect keener than ours and a capacity for loving greater than ours. In the most literal sense of the word, he is unique. Uncreated, infinite, totally other, he surpasses and transcends all human concepts, considerations, and expectations. He is beyond anything we can intellectualize or imagine. Thus, Jesus is a scandal to men and women everywhere, because he cannot be comprehended by the rational, finite mind.

BRENNAN MANNING

WE MUST LEARN FROM GOD

JOHN 4:10 NLT
Jesus replied, "If you only knew the gift God
has for you and who I am, you would ask me,
and I would give you living water."

Our nature can't contemplate heavenly things by its own strength. We must learn from God what we should think of Him. We have no source of knowledge but God Himself. You might be as well trained in secular philosophy as possible, and you may have lived a life of righteousness. But, although all of this will add to your mental satisfaction, it won't help you know God. Moses was adopted as the queen's son. He was instructed in all the Egyptians' wisdom. Moreover, out of loyalty to his race, Moses avenged the Hebrew by slaying the Egyptian who wronged him. Yet he didn't know the God who blessed his fathers. . . . Then he heard the voice of God, asked His name, and learned His nature. Despite all this he couldn't have known anything except through God Himself. We, in the same way, must confine whatever we say about God to the words He has spoken to us about Himself.

HILARY OF POITIERS

THIRSTY FOR LIVING WATER

JOHN 4:10 NIV

Jesus answered her, "If you knew the gift of God and who it is that asks you for a drink, you would have asked him and he would have given you living water."

The soul can also manifest physical symptoms of need. I like to think of it this way: Just like my stomach growls when I'm hungry for physical food, my spirit tends to growl when I'm in need of spiritual food. When a checker at the grocery store seems overtly irritable or grouchy, I sometimes grin and think to myself, "I bet her kids woke up before she had a chance to have her quiet time!" I can certainly assure you that my personality is distinctively different when I haven't had the time I need with the Lord. My soul can do some pretty fierce growling!

How about you? Does your hungry soul ever manifest physical symptoms such as irritability, selfish ambitions, anger, impure thoughts, envy, resentments, and eruptions of lust?

Here's a similar analogy. When a soul is thirsty for the Living Water (John 4), just as my mouth gets dry when I am thirsty, my spiritual mouth gets dry when I need the satisfying refreshment only God can bring.

BETH MOORE

THE WORD MADE FLESH

JOHN 4:11–12 NASB

She said to Him, "Sir, You have nothing to draw with
and the well is deep; where then do You get that
living water? You are not greater than our father
Jacob, are You, who gave us the well, and
drank of it himself and his sons and his cattle?"

He is the Word-made-flesh, the Incarnation of the compassion of the Father. He is Messiah, Savior, dreamer and storyteller, servant, friend, and parable of God. Close to the brokenhearted, he speaks words of comfort; he revives the crushed in spirit with words of consolation. Rescuing drunks, scalawags, and ragamuffins, he is the Shepherd who feeds, leads, and searches out.

He is prophet, poet, and troublemaker, the scourge of hypocrites and authority figures who use religion to control others, sending them sagging under great burdens of regulations, watching them stumble and refusing to offer assistance. He excoriates the perverted spirit of legalism and the smug religious bureaucrats who condemn simple folks who for good reasons have broken bad religious laws. When he looks out at the bedraggled, beat-up, bollixed, and burnt-out, his heart overflows with unspeakable tenderness.

BRENNAN MANNING

PAYING ATTENTION TO THE SOURCE

JOHN 4:13–14 NIV
Jesus answered, "Everyone who drinks this water will be thirsty again, but whoever drinks the water I give him will never thirst. Indeed, the water I give him will become in him a spring of water welling up to eternal life."

Consider the lilies of the field, how they grow; they simply are! Think of the sea, the air, the sun, the stars and the moon—all these are, and what a ministration they exert. So often we mar God's designed influence through us by our self-conscious effort to be consistent and useful. Jesus says that there is only one way to develop spiritually, and that is by concentration on God. "Do not bother about being of use to others; believe on Me"—pay attention to the Source, and out of you will flow rivers of living water. . . .

The people who influence us most are not those who buttonhole us and talk to us, but those who live their lives like the stars in heaven and the lilies in the field, perfectly simply and unaffectedly. Those are the lives that mould us.

If you want to be of use to God, get rightly related to Jesus Christ and He will make you of use unconsciously every minute you live.

OSWALD CHAMBERS

GOD IS WITHIN US

JOHN 4:13–14 NCV

*Jesus answered, "Everyone who drinks this water
will be thirsty again, but whoever drinks the water
I give will never be thirsty. The water I give
will become a spring of water gushing up inside
that person, giving eternal life."*

The meaning and symbolism of water in the Bible run deep—no pun intended. God's Spirit is ever present in our midst to refresh us, cleanse us, and strengthen us for the journey. He is the eternal spring that never runs dry. . . .

The Holy Spirit of God living with you is a secret fountain of life giving water. People don't realize the depth of God's Spirit in residence within your soul. Through the Holy Spirit, God has come to live inside you. There's no way to overstate the powerful implications of that startling truth. Why should we look outside for help when trouble comes? Almighty God is among us and within us. He is the source of living water, springing up into eternal life.

DAVID JEREMIAH

A CONTINUALLY FLOWING FOUNTAIN

JOHN 4:13 NASB

Jesus answered and said to her, "Everyone who drinks of this water will thirst again."

Every one that drinketh of this water. . . . He distinguishes between the use of the two kinds of water; that the one serves the body, and only for a time, while the power of the other gives perpetual vigour to the soul. For, as the body is liable to decay, so the aids by which it is supported must be frail and transitory. That which quickens the soul cannot but be eternal. Again, the words of Christ are not at variance with the fact, that believers, to the very end of life, burn with desire of more abundant grace. For he does not say that, from the very first day, we drink so as to be fully satisfied, but only means that the Holy Spirit is a continually flowing fountain; and that, therefore, there is no danger that they who have been renewed by spiritual grace shall be dried up.

JOHN CALVIN

THE GREAT PURCHASE OF CHRIST

JOHN 4:13–14 NIV
*Jesus answered, "Everyone who drinks this
water will be thirsty again, but whoever drinks
the water I give him will never thirst. Indeed,
the water I give him will become in him a
spring of water welling up to eternal life."*

The Spirit of Christ is given to his church and people
forever, everlastingly to influence them and dwell in
them. The Holy Spirit is the great purchase of Christ.
God the Father is the person of whom the purchase is
made; God the Son is the person who makes the purchase; and the Holy Spirit is the gift purchased. The sum
of all those good things in this life, and the life to come,
which are purchased for the church is the Holy Spirit.
And as this is the great purchase, so it is the great promise of God and Christ. Acts 2:33, "Having received of the
Father the promise of the Holy Ghost, he hath shed forth
this, which ye now see and hear." And this great purchase
of Christ is forever given to his church.

JONATHAN EDWARDS

THE HUNGER OF OUR SOULS

JOHN 4:13–15 NLT

Jesus replied, "People soon become thirsty again after drinking this water. But the water I give them takes away thirst altogether. It becomes a perpetual spring within them, giving them eternal life."

"Please, sir," the woman said, "give me some of that water! Then I'll never be thirsty again, and I won't have to come here to haul water."

Many spiritual functions parallel physical functions. As our bodies hunger and thirst, so do our souls. But our souls need spiritual food and water. The woman confused the two kinds of water, perhaps because no one had ever talked with her about her spiritual hunger and thirst before. We would not think of depriving our bodies of food and water when they hunger or thirst. Why then would we deprive our souls? The living Word, Jesus Christ, and the written Word, the Bible, can satisfy our hungry and thirsty souls.

LIFE APPLICATION BIBLE

OVERFLOWING HOPE

JOHN 4:27–29 NIV

*Just then his disciples returned and were surprised
to find him talking with a woman. But no
one asked, "What do you want?" or "Why are
you talking with her?" Then, leaving her water jar,
the woman went back to the town and said to
the people, "Come, see a man who told me
everything I ever did. Could this be the Christ?"*

The Samaritan woman grasped what He said with a
fervor that came from an awareness of her real need.

The transaction was fascinating. She had come with a
bucket. He sent her back with a spring of living water.

She had come as a reject. He sent her back being
accepted by God Himself. . . .

She came laden with questions. He sent her back as a
source for answers.

She came living a life of quiet desperation. She ran back
overflowing with hope.

The disciples missed it all. It was lunchtime for them.

RAVI ZACHARIAS

OPEN YOUR SOUL

EPHESIANS 1:17–19 NRSV

I pray that the God of our Lord Jesus Christ, the Father of glory, may give you a spirit of wisdom and revelation as you come to know him, so that, with the eyes of your heart enlightened, you may know what is the hope to which he has called you, what are the riches of his glorious inheritance among the saints, and what is the immeasurable greatness of his power for us who believe, according to the working of his great power.

Throw open all the windows of your soul to the influence of Jesus. By prayer, thought, and action, let His divine power move in and through your life; and be sure that a mighty work is within His power and your possibility. Not that of lifting you into ordinary spiritual vitality, but of transforming you through and through with His Spirit.

WILLIAM LAWRENCE

PICTURES OF
CHRIST'S RETURN

"Yes, I am coming soon." Amen.
Come, Lord Jesus.
REVELATION 22:20 NIV

PICTURES OF CHRIST'S RETURN

We wait expectantly. We balance busyness with watchfulness. We plan in case He tarries and live in anticipation. Jesus' parables about His return urge us to practice vigorous work and constant vigilance. He selected a noteworthy event like a wedding and the everyday relationship between a landowner and tenants to illustrate the tension between watching and waiting. Attempting to maintain the balance proves to be a challenge for all of us.

In the Lord's Supper, the morphing of elements provides a healthy reminder and lesson. Not only does bread become body and the cup become blood, but also the looking back becomes looking forward. In the taking, we remember Him and His death until He comes. We glance back in remembrance and look forward with renewed anticipation.

The virgins at the wedding and the tenants at work also remind us that every day could be the day. Working while we wait becomes a daily covenant of obedience as we eagerly await Christ's return.

WATCH

MATTHEW 25:1–4 ESV

"Then the kingdom of heaven will be like ten virgins
who took their lamps and went to meet the bridegroom.
Five of them were foolish, and five were wise. For when
the foolish took their lamps, they took no oil with them,
but the wise took flasks of oil with their lamps."

W atch" does not mean look out the window at night. It does not mean go up on a mountain and wait. Even the wise virgins slept when it was time to sleep. Watch means: Be spiritually awake! Be alive and alert to Jesus Christ and the Holy Spirit that He gives now. Use all the means God has given you to know Him and love Him and trust Him. Be filled with the oil of faith and joy and hope.

Let this thought govern your life: Jesus Christ came to betroth a people to Himself at the price of His own blood. If I am a part of that betrothed people by faith in Jesus, He will come to me (and all who believe in Him) and say, "Come, O faithful bride, enter into My gardens and into My chambers and learn now for eternity what the dim shadows of earthly pleasures were all about."

JOHN PIPER

I NEVER KNEW YOU!

MATTHEW 25:10 ESV
*"And while they were going to buy, the bridegroom
came, and those who were ready went in with him
to the marriage feast, and the door was shut."*

The climax of the story comes at the end of verse 10
when the door is shut. There is a grim finality about
this shutting of the banquet door that is unlikely to reflect
the bonhomie, or general atmosphere of geniality, usually
associated with a village wedding ceremony. No doubt in
real life the pathetic appeal of the foolish girls in verse 11
would have met with a more sympathetic response. But
the story is increasingly losing the contours of everyday life
and taking on the dimensions of the final judgment. . . .
The bridegroom answers them in almost the same words
as directed to evildoers on the day of final judgment, as
given in [Matthew] 7:23: "I never knew you!" Their
unreadiness, the story suggests, consisted not in what they
did or did not do, but in a failure of relationship. And so,
as in Jesus' teaching in 7:21–23, what ultimately decides
whether one is inside or outside the door is being known
by the bridegroom.

R. T. FRANCE

WE WILL RISE

1 THESSALONIANS 4:16–17 NASB
*For the Lord Himself will descend from heaven
with a shout, with the voice of the archangel
and with the trumpet of God, and the dead in Christ
will rise first. Then we who are alive and
remain will be caught up together with them
in the clouds to meet the Lord in the air, and
so we shall always be with the Lord.*

What an odd Sunday afternoon I had. My mother-in-law recently purchased a family grave plot at a cemetery called Forest Lawn. However, she would not sign the papers until Ken and I looked at the lot and gave our approval. . . .

While the realtor and my mother-in-law conferred over the papers, I looked around at the hundreds of tombstones. It suddenly struck me that I was sitting on the exact spot where my body will rise, should I die before Christ comes. Sitting on that grassy hillside did more to ignite the reality of the Resurrection than hearing sermons or reading essays on the subject.

The Resurrection is not something to be spiritualized away. One day actual spirits will return to actual graves and reunite to rise. Dead men, one day, shall live, hallelujah!

JONI EARECKSON TADA

WITH HIM FOREVER

JOHN 12:26 NRSV
"Whoever serves me must follow me,
and where I am, there will my servant be also.
Whoever serves me, the Father will honor."

As I get older, I find that I appreciate God and people and good and lovely and noble things more and more intensely; so it is pure delight to think that this enjoyment will continue and increase in some form (what form, God knows, and I am content to wait and see), literally forever. . . .

We cannot visualize heaven's life and the wise man will not try to do so. Instead he will dwell on the doctrine of heaven, where the redeemed will find all their heart's desire: joy with their Lord, joy with his people, and joy in the ending of all frustration and distress and in the supply of all wants. . . .

What shall we do in heaven? Not lounge around but worship, work, think, and communicate, enjoying activity, beauty, people, and God. First and foremost, however, we shall see and love Jesus, our Savior, Master, and Friend.

J. I. PACKER

WE WILL BE CHANGED

PHILIPPIANS 3:20–21 NCV
*But our homeland is in heaven, and we are waiting for
our Savior, the Lord Jesus Christ, to come from heaven.
By his power to rule all things, he will change our simple
bodies and make them like his own glorious body.*

The bodies of the just must arise again, because of
that similitude, that must be betwixt the body of
the Lord Jesus Christ and the bodies of the saints. "When
he shall appear, we shall be like him"(1 John 3:2).

Now, I say, it would be very strange to me if Christ
should be raised, ascended, and glorified in that body; and
yet that his people should be with him, not otherwise
than in their spirits.

And hence it is that the scripture saith, He "shall
change our vile body, that it may be fashioned like unto
his glorious body" (Philippians 3:21). And hence it is
again, that the day of Christ is said to be the day of the
manifestation of the sons of God, and of the redemption
of our body (Romans 8:21–24), for then shall the saints
of God not only be, but appear as their Savior, being
delivered from their graves, as he is from his, and glorified
in their bodies, as he is in his.

JOHN BUNYAN

Like a Thief in the Night

Mark 13:35–37 niv

*"Therefore keep watch because you do not
know when the owner of the house will come
back—whether in the evening, or at midnight,
or when the rooster crows, or at dawn. If he comes
suddenly, do not let him find you sleeping. What
I say to you, I say to everyone: 'Watch!'"*

Jesus told the disciples a set of interlaced parables about
being ready for His return. The point of each dealt
with watchfulness and doing what Christ assigns us to
do. Christ wants His people to be ready and waiting.
No matter whether you're a pretribulationalist, a post-
tribulationalist, an amillennialist, a dispensationalist, or
have no clue what any of those mean, Christ is coming
back. Every eye will see Him. Some things about God's
ways make me grin . . . like the way He knows our tendency to play amateur prophet. He puts all of us in our
date-setting places by basically saying, "The only thing I'll
tell you about My next visit is that you won't be expecting Me." The urgency is to be ready at all times.

Beth Moore and Dale McCleskey

DON'T BE FOUND SLEEPING

MARK 13:34–37 NKJV

*"It is like a man going to a far country, who left
his house and gave authority to his servants, and
to each his work, and commanded the doorkeeper
to watch. Watch therefore, for you do not know
when the master of the house is coming . . . lest,
coming suddenly, he find you sleeping. And what
I say to you, I say to all: Watch!"*

Some feel that *the doorkeeper* is only part of the 'scenery'
of the parable, and therefore requires no special exe-
gesis. But there is some evidence to show that the simile
of the 'porter' was used by the early church for those
engaged in Christian ministry. The master of the house,
when he arrives after his long absence, must not find us
sleeping, but doing our duty and carrying out the particular task which he has left to us. . . .

[Verse 37] shows us that the command is generalized,
not directed only at the Christian ministry or indeed at
any group or class within the church. Further, it may be
a clear indication that Jesus Himself did not necessarily
expect that His second coming would be in the near
future, as many modern expositors assume rather than
prove. The whole tenor of this parable suggests a long
absence.

R. A. COLE

TRANSFORMED

***

1 JOHN 3:2 NIV

Dear friends, now we are children of God, and
what we will be has not yet been made known.
But we know that when he appears, we shall
be like him, for we shall see him as he is.

We do know this, *that when he appears, we shall be like him, for we shall see him as he is.* The sequence is clear. First, he will appear; in consequence, we will see him as he is; and so we shall be like him. . . . The new nature, which we assumed at our conversion, was 'created to be like God in true righteousness and holiness' (Ephesians 4:24; *cf.* Colossians 3:10). And since that day, . . . the Holy Spirit has been transfiguring us 'into his likeness with ever-increasing glory' (2 Corinthians 3:18; *cf.* 1 John 2:6). In this latter passage the transformation is said to be due to the fact that 'with unveiled faces' we 'all reflect the Lord's glory.' This being so, it is understandable that when we see him as he is, and not our face only but his too will be unveiled, we will be finally and completely like him, including our bodies (Philippians 3:21; *cf.* 1 Corinthians 15:49).

JOHN R. W. STOTT

THE FACE OF GOD

1 JOHN 4:12 NASB
No one has seen God at any time;
if we love one another, God abides in us,
and His love is perfected in us.

God is invisible. He can't be seen with eyes but with the heart. If we want to see the sun, we should purge the physical eye. In the same way, if we want to see God, we must purify the eye that we see God with. Where is this eye? Listen to the Gospel of Matthew: "Blessed are the pure in heart, for they shall see God." We shouldn't imagine God according to what we want to see. . . . But imagine this if you want to see God: "God is love." What sort of face does love have? What shape does it take? What stature? What feet or hands? No one can say. And yet it has feet that carry people to church. It has hands that reach out to the poor. It has eyes that show us those in need. . . . These aren't separate parts of love, but bring complete understanding and sight to those who have it. Live in love, and love will live in you.

AUGUSTINE

Eternal Happiness

1 Thessalonians 4:17 NRSV
*Then we who are alive, who are left, will be caught
up in the clouds together with them to meet the Lord
in the air; and so we will be with the Lord forever.*

I n heaven are many mansions, and of different degrees
of dignity. The glory of the saints above will be in some
proportion to their eminency in holiness and good works
here. . . . It will be no damp to the happiness of those who
have lower degrees of happiness and glory, that there are
others advanced in glory above them: for all shall be perfectly happy, every one shall be perfectly satisfied. . . .

If the saints knew that there would be an end to their
happiness, though at never so great a distance, yet it would
be a great damp to their joy. The greater the happiness is,
so much the more uncomfortable would the thoughts of
an end be, and so much the more joyful will it be to think
that there will be no end. The saints will surely know that
there will be no more danger of their happiness coming
to an end, than there will be that the being of God will
come to an end.

Jonathan Edwards

RESPONSIBILITY

MATTHEW 24:45 NLT
*"Who is a faithful, sensible servant, to whom
the master can give the responsibility of managing
his household and feeding his family?"*

Who then is the faithful . . . servant. . . . The disciples
used to reckon they were unfairly treated unless
they were exempt from the common lot and given long
preference over all others. Now when they are given
terms that are not very attractive or pleasant, they look in
all directions in their astonishment. The object of Christ's
reply is that if any of the ordinary people should keep
watch it is intolerable that the Apostles should be dozing.
. . . Since they have a higher rank of honour granted
them, a greater burden falls on them. Therefore they are
particularly taught to exercise faith and prudence. Hence
any may learn who are called to the responsibility of
office that they are more obliged to fulfil their tasks without slackness, and, with all their care and effort, to strive
to do their duty.

JOHN CALVIN

LISTEN TO THE LORD

MATTHEW 24:45–46 NIV
"Who then is the faithful and wise servant,
whom the master has put in charge of the servants
in his household to give them their food at the
proper time? It will be good for that servant whose
master finds him doing so when he returns."

Let everyone, then, wisely receive the admonitions of the Master, before the season of the Savior's mercy passes by—a season that is now in blossom, as long as the human race is spared. For the reason we are spared is that we may be converted rather than condemned. Only God knows when the end of the world will come; nevertheless, now is the time for faith. Whether any of us here will be around at the end of the world, I do not know; perhaps the end will not find us. Even so, our own end is very near to each of us, since we are mortal. No doubt through our frailness we walk daily in fear of the accidents inherent in life; and even if these accidents do not occur, time goes on. However long we may be spared, in the end, old age comes, and there is no way of putting that off. For that reason, we must listen to the Lord.

AUGUSTINE

HE WILL RETURN

MATTHEW 24:46–51 ESV

*"Blessed is that servant whom his master will
find so doing when he comes. Truly, I say to you,
he will set him over all his possessions. But if
that wicked servant says to himself, 'My master is
delayed,' and begins to beat his fellow servants and
eats and drinks with drunkards, the master of that
servant will come on a day when he does not expect
him and at an hour he does not know and will cut
him in pieces and put him with the hypocrites."*

Jesus tells a story of two slaves who work for an absentee master. One slave is good and faithful, and the other is evil and faithless. The good slave represents believers who will be on the earth before the Lord's return, while the evil servant represents unbelievers. [John MacArthur points out that] every person in the world holds his life, his possessions, and his abilities in trust from God, and they will all be held accountable to the Lord for what they have done with that trust. In the case of this evil servant, the dominant attitude is one of calloused procrastination. He doesn't believe the master is going to come back anytime soon, so he has no motivation to cease doing evil. Christ's words warn him to be careful because he doesn't know the schedule.

DAVID JEREMIAH

WAIT FOR YOUR LORD

MATTHEW 24:46–47 NRSV
"Blessed is that slave whom his master will find at work when he arrives. Truly I tell you, he will put that one in charge of all his possessions."

In any case not because we are what we really are today, but that the people here are seen in an entirely different perspective, namely, as those who are never anything in themselves, as those who are already covered by the eternal peace and eternal salvation of God, as the persons over whom the approach of the new heaven and the new earth has already won power, that is, as the people in the perspective of the future of God, in which the suffering, struggling, dying God of human history is revealed as the First and the Last, to whom the kingdom belonged from the beginning. And because Christ knows of this future out of his mysterious, eternal knowledge, for that reason he blesses them [the servants]; blessed as those to whom God will someday come, and who live today totally for this coming, this being overpowered by God. Blessed are those who wait, blessed are those who watch and wait. Be like those who wait for their Lord! Blessed are those servants whom the Lord finds watching when he comes.

DIETRICH BONHOEFFER

HIS PARABLES

THE MASTER SERVANT

LUKE 12:37–38 ESV

"Blessed are those servants whom the master
finds awake when he comes. Truly, I say to you,
he will dress himself for service and have them
recline at table, and he will come and serve them.
If he comes in the second watch, or in the third,
and finds them awake, blessed are those servants!"

I refer to this as a stunning parable because it portrays the returning Christ as a "master" who nevertheless "will gird himself to serve, and have them [his servants] recline at the table, and will come up and wait on them" (Luke 12:37). This takes the breath away. The one we wait for, who will come in the clouds with the holy angels and the glory of His Father and terrify the nations—this one will magnify His greatness in mercy and servanthood and make himself the servant of our joy forever. Not even after the second coming will He be "served by human hands, as though He needed anything, since He Himself gives to all life and breath and all things" (Acts 17:25).

JOHN PIPER

THE GRACE-GIVER

LUKE 12:37–38 NLT

*"There will be special favor for those who are ready
and waiting for his return. I tell you, he himself will
seat them, put on an apron, and serve them as they
sit and eat! He may come in the middle of the night
or just before dawn. But whenever he comes, there
will be special favor for his servants who are ready!"*

And perhaps most glorious of all is the jealousy with
which He will magnify His grace. He will not share
the glory of being the grace-giver. Peter tells us simply,
"Set your hope fully on the grace that will be brought to
you at the revelation of Jesus Christ" (1 Peter 1:13). And
what will that grace look like? Jesus pictured it in a parable: "Blessed are those servants whom the master finds
awake when he comes. Truly, I say to you, he will dress
himself for service and have them recline at table, and
he will come and serve them" (Luke 12:37). It is the
grace of God's being our "Servant"—the Giver—even to
eternity.

JOHN PIPER

WE ARE WHAT WE BELIEVE

MATTHEW 16:26 NRSV

*"For what will it profit them if they gain the
whole world but forfeit their life? Or what
will they give in return for their life?"*

One who delights in the world, who is enticed by
flattering and deceiving earthly pleasures wants to
remain in the world a long time. . . . Since the world hates
Christians, why do you love that which hates you? And
why don't you follow Christ instead, who both redeemed
you and loves you? John, in his epistle, cries and urges us
not to follow fleshly desires and love the world. "Love not
the world," he says, ". . . the world shall pass away, and the
lust thereof; but he who doeth the will of God abideth for
ever, even as God abideth for ever." Instead, beloved, let
us be prepared for the will of God with a sound mind, a
firm faith, and strong virtue. Laying aside the fear of
death, let us think on the eternal life to come. Through
this knowledge, let us demonstrate that we are what we
believe. . . . Then we won't delay or resist the Lord on the
day He calls us to Himself.

CYPRIAN

NEW LIFE

HEBREWS 10:37 NASB
For yet in a very little while,
He who is coming will come, and will not delay.

Scholars note that the Hebrew Scriptures have very few clear references to a fulfilled life with God beyond the grave. Christians now, however, connect their own resurrection with that of Jesus, a rising to life that is described not as an ordinary act, not even an ordinary "resurrection." Instead, what happened in and to the risen Jesus is pictured as something without analogy or comparison. It is something wholly new. He is the first fruit of the new creation.

Today stained-glass images, trumpets, the company of fellow believers, and clear readings of Scripture all work to reinforce the faith of those who believe that their new life comes with Christ's. But on the unending pilgrimage of faith and hope, the resurrection experience is not confined to one day, one story, one mood. It occurs every morning, on every day called the Lord's Day, and upon every act of turning from old to new, of accepting the new life that brings its own graces.

MARTIN MARTY AND MICAH MARTY

HIS PARABLES

SERVICE TO GOD

MATTHEW 25:32–33 NIV
*"All the nations will be gathered before him, and he
will separate the people one from another as a shepherd
separates the sheep from the goats. He will put the
sheep on his right and the goats on his left."*

There is of course a sense in which no one can give
to God anything which is not already His; and if it is
already His what have you given? But since it is only too
obvious that we can withhold ourselves, our wills and
hearts, from God, we can, in that sense, also give them.
What is His by right and would not exist for a moment
if it ceased to be His (as the song is the singer's), He has
nevertheless made ours in such a way that we can freely
offer it back to Him. "Our wills are ours to make them
Thine." And as all Christians know there is another way
of giving to God; every stranger whom we feed or clothe
is Christ. And this apparently is Gift-love to God whether
we know it or not. Love Himself can work in those who
know nothing of Him. The "sheep" in the parable had no
idea either of the God hidden in the prisoner whom they
visited or of the God hidden in themselves when they
made the visit.

C. S. LEWIS

SERVING THE LORD JESUS

*"Then the King will say to those on His right,
'Come, you who are blessed of My Father, inherit the
kingdom prepared for you from the foundation of the
world. For I was hungry, and you gave Me something
to eat; I was thirsty, and you gave Me something to
drink; I was a stranger, and you invited Me in.'"*

L ord, when did we see you hungry and feed you?"
Those declared blessed at the Last Judgment will have
no memory of meeting Jesus in those whom they fed,
sheltered, and comforted. They won't remember because
in those moments when urgent need surfaced, they forgot themselves. In unselfconscious freedom, they responded
to human need without seeking to be noticed . . . At the
Last Judgment, they'll be bewildered to learn that the
befuddled old man shuffling around in his shabby apart-
ment, thick-tongued and mumbling about a prescription
he needed from the pharmacy, was the Master. It's liber-
ating to learn that we don't have to recognize Jesus in the
least brother or sister or bestow some Christ-like quality
on the derelict in the doorway. It's also demanding, however. The horizons of Christian concern broaden beyond
the morally upright, the potential convert, and the good-
natured slob.

BRENNAN MANNING

THE GOLDEN RULE

MATTHEW 25:34–35 NIV

"Then the King will say to those on his right, 'Come, you who are blessed by my Father; take your inheritance, the kingdom prepared for you since the creation of the world. For I was hungry and you gave me something to eat, I was thirsty and you gave me something to drink, I was a stranger and you invited me in.'"

In the parable of the sheep and the goats, Jesus illustrated how our passionate good deeds go much further than the people for whom we do them. . . .

It's interesting that Jesus uses down-and-outers to illustrate that passionate service to others is, in fact, ministry to Him. Perhaps it's because we find it difficult to serve people who are dirty, disreputable, or potentially dangerous to us; it's easier to be passionate about helping people whom we consider deserving. But as Jesus explained in the Sermon on the Mount, it's not up to us to make those kinds of evaluations. As long as the one who crosses our path is one who was created and loved by God, then we can be certain we must serve and love him too. And however we would wish to be treated, we can be certain we must treat that person the same way.

That principle, of course, is known as the golden rule.

DAVID JEREMIAH